BRANCH LINE TO CHEDDAR

including the Wrington Vale Light Railway

Vic Mitchell and Keith Smith

MP Middleton Press

Published February 1997
First reprint February 2001

ISBN 1 873793 90 1

© Middleton Press, 1997

Design Deborah Esher

Published by
    Middleton Press
    Easebourne Lane
    Midhurst, West Sussex
    GU29 9AZ
Tel: 01730 813169
Fax: 01730 812601

Printed & bound by Biddles Ltd,
    Guildford and Kings Lynn

CONTENTS

INDEX

ACKNOWLEDGEMENTS

We are very grateful for the help received from those mentioned in the photographic credits and also for the assistance given by W.R.Burton (Mowat Collection), J.Cooper, G.Croughton, P.Davey, P.Hay, J.B.Horne, N.Langridge, C.Maggs, A.C.Mott, D. Trevor Rowe, L.W.Rowe, Mr.D & Dr.S.Salter and our ever helpful wives.

Map of the route and adjacent lines as in 1930. (Railway Magazine)

GEOGRAPHICAL SETTING

From Witham to Cranmore the lines climbs steeply, mainly on clay subsoil, and reaches the southern border of the Mendip Hills where the limestone beds outcrop almost vertically. This has permitted quarrying to a great depth resulting in long-term heavy rail traffic.

West of Cranmore, the route falls almost continuously to the small city of Wells. It is at the foot of the Mendips from Shepton Mallet to Axbridge where it rises and turns north to pass through the western end of the hills in Shuteshelve Tunnel. For most of its length, the railway was constructed on clays but was sufficiently close to the limestone mass to serve a number of quarries. Caves in the hills have attracted tourists and thus generated rail revenue in times past.

From the tunnel to a point north of Sandford the route descends, mainly on clay. At Sandford there is further limestone outcropping which once gave rise to rail traffic. The remainder of the line to Yatton was fairly level, being mostly on the alluvium of the River Yeo, now known as the Congresbury Yeo.

Wrington Vale Light Railway

This took an undulating course climbing gently up the side of the Yeo Valley to Burrington, from where it descended and then climbed again to Blagdon station. The village is situated on the northern slope of the Mendips but the terminus was built well below it. Most of the branch was constructed on clay.

The maps are to the scale of 25ins to 1 mile, unless otherwise stated.

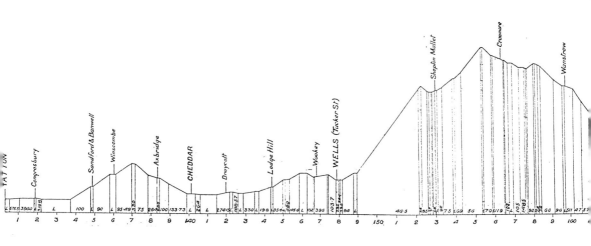

1870

Miles.	Fares.			Down.	1,2,3	1&2	1&2	1&2	1&2	Miles.	From Glastonbury, see pag 37.	1&2	1&2	1&2	1&2	1&2	1&2	
	1 cl.	2 cl.	3 cl.	Temple St. Sta.,	mrn	mrn	aft	aft	aft	aft			mrn	mrn	non	aft	aft	aft	
	s. d.	s. d.	s. d.	Bristol ..dep	8 30	1120	1235	3 45	6 0	8 40		Wells ....dep	7 55	9 35	12 0	1 10	5 40	7 50	
5½	1 2	0 11	0 5½	Bourton	8 44	....	....	....	....	8 53	3½	Lodge Hill	8 4	....	....	1 21	5 48	7 59	
8	1 8	1 4	0 8	Nailsea	8 52	....	....	6 18	9 0		5¾	Draycott	8 12	....	1213	1 30	....	8 7	
12	2 6	2 0	1 0	Yatton ..arr	9 5	1145	1258	4 10	6 31	9 10	8	Cheddar	8 20	9 53	1222	1 39	6 2	8 15	
16	2 6	2 0	1 4	Clevedon dep	8 48	1116	1215	3 28	6 15	8 38	9½	Axbridge	8 26	10 0	1228	1 45	6 8	8 21	
—	....	....	....	Yatton ....dep	9 25	1153	1 10	4 15	6 32	9 12	12	Winscombe	8 35	....	1240	1 56	6 19	8 30	
13½	3 0	2 3	1 1½	Congresbury ..	9 30	1158	1 15	4 20	6 37	9 19	13	Saudford & Banwell	8 41	1012	1246	2 3	....	8 36	
16½	3 6	2 9	1 4½	Sandford & Banwell	9 42	1210	1 27	4 32	6 46	9 28	16	Congresbury ..	8 50	....	....	2 14	....	8 45	
17½	3 9	3 0	1 5½	Winscombe	9 47	1215	1 32	4 37	6 52	9 34	17½	Yatton 8, 7 arr	8 55	1023	1253	2 19	6 30	8 50	
20	4 0	3 0	1 8	Axbridge	10 0	1228	1 45	4 50	7 1	9 43	21½	Clevedon arr	9 26	1035	....	2 41	6 52	9 25	
21½	4 0	3 4	1 9½	Cheddar	10 6	1235	1 52	4 57	7 8	9 50	—	Yatton ..dep	9 0	1025	1257	2 15	6 42	8 52	
23½	4 6	3 6	1 11½	Draycott	1014	1242	2 1	5 6	7 16	9 58	21½	Nailsea	9 9	....	1 6	....	6 52	9 0	
26	5 0	3 9	2 2	Lodge Hill	1022	1249	2 10	5 15	7 24	10 6	24	Bourtn [172 a	9 15	....	1 14	....	6 57	9 8	
29½	6 4	0 2	5½	Wells 14, 37 ..arr	1030	1255	2 20	5 25	7 30	1012	29½	Bristol 8, 15,	9 30	1050	1 35	2 50	7 15	9 30	

CHEDDAR VALLEY BRANCH.—Bristol and Exeter.

No Sunday Trains.

Extra Trains, see page 7. Extra Trains, see page 9.

To Wells from the East

The Frome - Yeovil section of the Wilts, Somerset & Weymouth Railway opened in 1856 and a branch from Witham to Shepton Mallet came into use on 9th November 1858. The remaining part of the East Somerset Railway between Shepton Mallet and Wells first saw traffic on 1st March 1862. The Acts for the two sections of the line were passed on 5th June 1856 and 27th July 1857 respectively. The branch was converted from broad to standard gauge in 1874, the year in which it came under the control of the Great Western Railway.

To Wells from the West

The Bristol & Exeter Railway opened its line south to Bridgwater in 1841 and provided a branch from Yatton to Clevedon in 1847. Its Act for a branch from Yatton to Wells was passed on 14th July 1864 and the line came into use in two stages - to Cheddar on 3rd August 1869 and to Wells on 5th April 1870. The route was altered from broad to standard gauge in November 1875 and became part of the GWR in January 1876.

To Wells from the South

Although not a subject of this book, the line must be considered as its presence at Wells prevented the joining of the two branches described above for 16 years. The Somerset Central Railway's Highbridge to Glastonbury line was extended to Wells on 15th March 1859 and was thus the first railway to that city. Its fan-shaped goods yard had to be crossed by the linking line and the Board of Trade refused to give consent for this until 1st January 1878. By that date, the SCR was part of the Somerset & Dorset Joint Railway.

The Blagdon Branch

A Light Railway Order for the construction of the Wrington Vale Light Railway was obtained in 1898. The line was built by the GWR and came into use on 4th December 1901. The Light Railway Act allowed for many economies to be made, such as not providing gates at level crossings or signals at the stations.

Closures

Passenger services were withdrawn from the Wrington Vale line on 14th September 1931 but freight continued to Blagdon until 1st November 1950 and to Wrington until 10th June 1963.

Witham-Yatton passenger trains ceased on 9th September 1963 but goods services ran to Wells until 13th July 1964 and a private siding was in use at Cheddar until 28th March 1969. Closure to freight traffic between Cheddar and Yatton took place on 1st October 1964. Stone traffic still continues from Merehead Quarry at the eastern end of the line.

Reopening

A steam centre was established at Cranmore in 1973 and East Somerset Railway passenger trains soon began to run westwards, reaching Merryfield Lane on 4th April 1980. A two mile long journey was possible from 23rd June 1985, when services were extended to Mendip Vale.

1910

YATTON, CHEDDAR, WELLS, and WITHAM (1st and 3rd class).—Great Western.

PASSENGER SERVICES

Prior to the union of the two branches at Wells, six trains were provided each way on both lines weekdays only, in most years. The designation of "down" for all trains to Wells continued after through working was established and until closure. Five to seven trains were operated on weekdays throughout the life of the route, although there were a few short workings and many through trains had a long wait at Wells in order to make reasonable connections at the junctions. There were some additional journeys on Saturdays in the later years.

Sunday services were introduced west of Wells in 1886 and east thereof in 1900, but there was seldom more than one train each way. Its main purpose was the conveyance of milk. The service ceased in the mid-1950s but was restored between Yatton and Wells in the final years, although it did not operate in the last 12 months.

Blagdon branch

Four trains each way were run from the opening until 1919 when the number was reduced to three. It was restored to four in March 1924 and a Sunday service was provided for the first time. This was an early morning trip, mainly for the carriage of milk. By the time of closure, there were two return journeys, weekdays only.

1935

YATTON, CHEDDAR, WELLS, and WITHAM.

Miles	Down.	Week Days. mrn	mrn	mrn	mrn	aft	aft	aft	aft	aft		Sn aft
—	**Yatton** dep.	8 0	9 52	..	1058	..	2 52	4 5	6 5	8 45	..	1 27
1½	Congresbury	8 5	9 57	..	11 2	..	2 56	4 9	6 9	8 49	..	1 31
4½	Sandford and Banwell	8 11	10 4	..	11 8	..	3 2	4 15	6 15	8 54	..	1 37
5½	Winscombe (Somerset)	8 15	10 8	..	1112	..	3 6	4 19	6 19	8 58	..	1 41
8	Axbridge	8 20	1014	..	1117	..	3 12	4 24	6 24	9 3	..	1 46
9¾	Cheddar	8 25	1019	..	1122	..	3 17	4A39	6 29	9 8	..	1 51
11¾	Draycott	8 30	1024	..	1127	..	3 22	4 44	6 34	9 12	..	1 55
14	Lodge Hill	8 35	1029	..	1132	..	3 27	4 49	6 45	9 17	..	2 7
16½	Wookey	8 41	1036	..	1138	..	3 32	4 55	6 51	9 23	..	2 11
17½	**Wells H** arr.	8 44	1039	..	1141	..	3 35	4 58	6 54	9 26	..	2 14
	dep.	9 9	..	11 1	..	1234	3 49	..	7 1	..	..	3 14
17¾	" (Priory Road) 1078	9 10	..	11 2	..	1235	3 50	..	7 2	..	..	3 15
22½	Shepton Mallet J 1076,	9 23	..	1116	..	1247	4 2	..	7 16	..	..	3 28
26	Cranmore [1077	9 31	..	1124	..	1256	4 10	..	7 24	..	..	3 36
29	Wanstrow	9 38	..	1131	..	1 3	4 17	..	7 31	..	..	3 43
31½	Witham 2, 8 arr.	9 44	..	1137	..	1 9	4 22	..	7 36	..	..	3 48

Miles	Up.	Week Days. mrn	mrn	mrn	mrn	aft	aft	aft	aft	aft	aft		Sun. aft	aft
—	**Witham** dep.	..	..	8 32	1151	1240	3 12	..	..	6 50	8 43	..	5 25	..
2½	Wanstrow	..	..	8 39	1158	1247	3 19	..	..	6 58	8 51	..	5 32	..
5½	Cranmore [1077	..	..	8 49	12 7	1257	3 28	..	..	7 8	9 1	..	5 39	..
9	Shepton Mallet J 1076,	..	8 47	8 58	1215	1 5	3 37	..	..	7 17	9 10	..	5 48	..
13¾	Wells (Priory Road) 1078	..	8 57	9 7	1224	1 14	3 46	.	..	7 26	9 20	..	5 58	..
14	" H arr.	..	8 58	9 8	1225	1 15	3 47	..	..	7 27	9 21	..	5 59	..
	dep.	7 15	9 0	9 43	1234	2 0	..	4 20	6 56	8 15		..	..	7 3
15	Wookey	7 18	..	9 47	1237	2 3	..	4 23	6 59	8 18		..	..	7 7
17½	Lodge Hill	7 23	9 7	9 58	1242	2 8	..	4 28	7 5	8 23		..	..	7 16
20	Draycott	7 27	9 11	10 3	1246	2 12	..	4 32	7 11	8 27	3rd class only.	..	..	7 21
22	Cheddar	7 31	9 16	10 8	1250	2 16	..	4 38	7 16	8 31		..	..	7 26
23½	Axbridge	7 35	9 21	1015	1254	2 20	..	4 42	7 23	8 35		..	..	7 32
26	Winscombe (Somerset)	7 40	9 26	1023	1259	2 25	..	4 47	7 29	8 40		..	..	7 39
27	Sandford and Banwell	7 43	9 30	1028	1 2	2 28	..	4 50	7 35	8 43		..	..	7 44
30	Congresbury	7 48	9 35	1036	1 7	2 33	..	4 56	7 46	8 50	..	..	..	7 51
31½	**Yatton 14, 20, 53** arr.	7 52	9 39	1040	1 11	2 37	..	5 0	7 50	8 54	..	..	..	7 54

YATTON, CHEDDAR, WELLS, and WITHAM

Miles		Week Days a.m	a.m		a.m		a.m	p.m		p.m	X	X		p.m		p.m			Sundays p.m		
	61 BRISTOL (T.M.) dep	..	7 25	..	9 0	..	10 38	..	..	1245	2 10	5 20	..	5 50	..	7 32	..	..	2 10	..	..
—	**Yatton** dep	6 55	7 58	..	9 45	..	11 12	..	..	1 10	2 47	5 47	..	6 10	..	8 8	..	..	2 30	..	..
1½	Congresbury	7 0	8 3	..	9 50	..	11 16	..	..	1 14	2 50	5 50	..	6 14	..	8 12	..	..	2 34	..	..
4½	Sandford and Banwell	7 6	8 9	..	9 57	..	11 22	..	..	1 20	2 56	5 56	..	6 20	..	8 18	..	..	2 40	..	..
5½	Winscombe (Somerset)	7 10	8 13	..	10 0	..	11 26	..	..	1 24	3 0	6 0	..	6 24	..	8 22	..	..	2 44	..	..
8	Axbridge	7 15	8 20	..	10 5	..	11 30	..	..	1 29	3 5	6 5	..	6 29	..	8 27	..	..	2 49	..	..
9¾	**Cheddar**	7 20	8 26	..	1010	..	11 35	..	..	1 34	3 12	6 10	..	6 34	..	8 32	..	..	2 54	..	..
11¾	Draycott	7 27	8 31	..	1015	..	11 40	..	..	1 39	3 17	6 14	..	6 39	..	8 37	..	..	2 58	..	..
14	Lodge Hill	7 32	8 36	..	1020	..	11 45	..	..	1 44	3 22	6 19	..	6 44	..	8 42	..	..	3 3	..	..
16½	Wookey	7 37	8 41	..	1025	..	11 50	..	..	1 49	3 27	6 24	..	6 49	..	8 47	..	..	3 7	..	..
17½	**Wells** (Tucker Street) arr	7 40	8 44	..	1028	..	11 53	..	..	1 53	3 31	6 28	..	6 52	..	8 50	..	..	3 10	..	..
	dep	..	9 5	..		..	..	12 7	..		3 49		..	7 0	..	..	..	..	3 17	..	..
17¾	" (Priory Road)	..	9 7	..	Sats. only	..	..	12 8	..	Sats. only	3 50	Except Saturdays	..	7 1	..	..	..	..	3 18	..	..
22½	Shepton Mallet L	..	9 20	..		..	..	1220	..		4 7		..	7 16	..	..	..	..	3 31	..	..
26	Cranmore	..	9 28	..		..	..	1228	..		4 18		..	7 24	..	..	..	..	3 39	..	..
29¼	Wanstrow	..	9 35	..		..	..	1235	..		4 25		..	7 31	..	..	..	..	3 46	..	..
31½	**Witham** arr	..	9 42	..		..	..	1242	..		4 31		..	7 36	..	..	..	..	3 51	..	..

Miles		Week Days a.m	a.m		a.m	X		p.m	p.m	p.m		p.m	p.m		p.m	p.m	p.m		Sundays p.m	p.m	
	Witham dep	..	..	..	8 25	10 20	..		1 30			3 37	X	..	6 49	..	9 20	..	5 28	..	..
2¼	Wanstrow	..	..	..	8 32	10 27	..		1 36		..	3 45		..	6 57	..	9 28	..	5 35	..	..
5½	Cranmore	..	..	..	8 39	10 37	..		1 43		..	3 53		..	7 7	..	9 38	..	5 42	..	..
9	Shepton Mallet L	..	..	..	8 47	10 44	..	Sats. only	1 51	Sats. only	..	4B 8	Except Sats.	..	7 16	..	9 46	..	5 50	..	..
13¾	**Wells** (Priory Road)	..	..	..	8 57	10 54	..		1 59		..	4 16		..	7 25	..	9 56	..	..	..	..
14	" (Tucker Street) arr	..	..	..	8 58	10 55	..		2 1		..	4 17		..	7 26	..	9 57	..	6 0	..	..
	dep	7 5	8 0	..	9 15	11 10	..	1210	2 5	2 57	..	4 22	7 0	..	..	8 15	..	..	..	7 20	..
15	Wookey	7 8	8 3	..	9 18	11 13	..	1213	2 8	2 59	..	4 25	7 3	..	..	8 18	..	..	..	7 23	..
17½	Lodge Hill	7 13	8 8	..	9 23	11 18	..	1218	2 13	3 4	..	4 30	7 8	..	..	8 23	..	..	..	7 29	..
19¾	Draycott	7 17	8 12	..	9 27	11 22	..	1222	2 17	3 8	..	4 34	7 13	..	..	8 27	..	..	..	7 33	..
21¾	**Cheddar**	7 21	8 16	..	9 31	11 26	..	1226	2 21	3 12	..	4 40	7 18	..	..	8 32	..	..	..	7 38	..
23½	Axbridge	7 25	8 22	..	9 36	11 30	..	1230	2 25	3 17	..	4 44	7 23	..	..	8 36	..	..	..	7 43	..
26	Winscombe (Somerset)	7 30	8 27	..	9 41	11 37	..	1235	2 30	3 22	..	4 49	7 29	..	..	8 41	..	..	..	7 49	..
27	Sandford and Banwell	7 33	8 30	..	9 44	11 40	..	1238	2 33	3 25	..	4 52	7 33	..	..	8 44	..	..	..	7 54	..
30	Congresbury	7 38	8 35	..	9 50	11 46	..	1244	2 38	3 30	..	4 58	7 40	..	..	8 50	..	..	..	8 0	..
31½	**Yatton** arr	7 42	8 39	..	9 54	11 50	..	1248	2 43	3 35	..	5 2	7 44	..	..	8 54	..	..	..	8 4	..
43½	61 BRISTOL (T.M.) arr	8 18	9 11	..	1013	12 11	..	1 26	3 12	4 0	..	5 30	8 6	..	..	9 51	..	..	..	8 25	..

B Arrive 4 1 p.m

L High Street Station: about 1 mile to Charlton Road Station

X Third class only, limited accommodation

1950

SOUTHERN RAILWAY

On SUNDAYS, AUGUST 6th & 20th.

Excursion

To SALISBURY,
(With its beautiful Cathedral and medieval buildings.)

WELLS

WOOKEY
(Visit the great three chambered cave, Museum, etc.)

AND

CHEDDAR
(Famed for its majestic Gorge and entrancing stalactite Caverns.)

DEPART	FROM				RETURN FARES, THIRD CLASS, TO:—			
					SALISBURY	WELLS	WOOKEY	CHEDDAR
a.m.					s. d.	s. d.	s. d.	s. d.
10 a 28	PORTSMOUTH HARBOUR	...	...	...	4/2	5/9	5/9	6/3
10 a 32	PORTSMOUTH & SOUTHSEA*	...	...	...				
10 37	FRATTON*	...	...	...				
10 46	COSHAM*	...	...	...	4/2	5/9	5/9	5/9
10 56	FAREHAM*	...	...	...	3/2	5/3	5/9	5/9
11 9	NETLEY*	...	...	...	3/2	5/3	5/3	5/9
11 14	SHOLING	...	...	...	2/8	5/3	5/3	5/9
11 17	WOOLSTON*	...	...	...	2/8	4/9	5/3	5/9
11 21	BITTERNE	...	...	...				
10 c 32	SWAYTHLING*	...	...	...	2/8	4/9	4/9	5/9
11 24	ST. DENYS*	...	...	...				
11 32	SOUTHAMPTON CENTRAL*	...	...	...				
11 c 0	EASTLEIGH	...	...	...	2/8	4/9	4/9	5/3
11 49	ROMSEY*	...	...	...	1/7	4/9	4/9	4/9
p.m.								
12 22	SALISBURY*	...	...	...	—	4/2	4/2	4/2

ARRIVE	AT				
12 19	SALISBURY	...	...	...	
2 6	WELLS (G.W.R.)	...	...	...	
2 19	WOOKEY (G.W.R.)	...	...	...	
2 36	CHEDDAR (G.W.R.)	...	...	...	

CHILDREN 3 AND UNDER 14 YEARS, HALF-FARE.

a—Special Early and Late Service of Buses.
c—Change at St. Denys in each direction.

* PARKING OF CARS—Passengers can park their cars at Stations marked * at a small charge. Apply at Booking Office.

RETURN TIMES, SAME DAY:—

ON			CHEDDAR (G.W.R.)	WOOKEY (G.W.R.)	WELLS (G.W.R.)	SALISBURY
			p.m.	p.m.	p.m.	p.m.
AUGUST 6th ... ...depart			6 40	6 56	7 6	8 58
AUGUST 20th ... ... „			6 55	7 12	7 24	9 8

IMPORTANT. TICKETS ARE LIMITED AND SHOULD BE PURCHASED IN ADVANCE AT THE STATIONS.

IMPORTANT NOTICE.
LATE FERRY SERVICE TO GOSPORT.

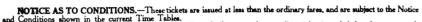

The Port of Portsmouth Steam Launch and Towing Co. Ltd. and the Gosport and Portsea Steam Launch Co. will provide late Ferry Services to Gosport in connection with the above Return Train at the usual charge of 1d. per passenger.

NOTICE AS TO CONDITIONS.—These tickets are issued at less than the ordinary fares, and are subject to the Notice and Conditions shown in the current Time Tables.

No luggage allowed except small handbags, luncheon baskets or other small articles intended for the passenger's personal use during the day.

On the RETURN journey passengers may take with them, free of charge, at Owner's Risk, goods not exceeding in the aggregate 60 lbs. which they may have purchased for their own use (not for sale).

DOGS, BICYCLES and PERAMBULATORS.—Reduced rates for return journey. FOLDED MAIL CARTS conveyed free.

Waterloo Station, S.E.1, July, 1939.   GILBERT S. SZLUMPER, General Manager.

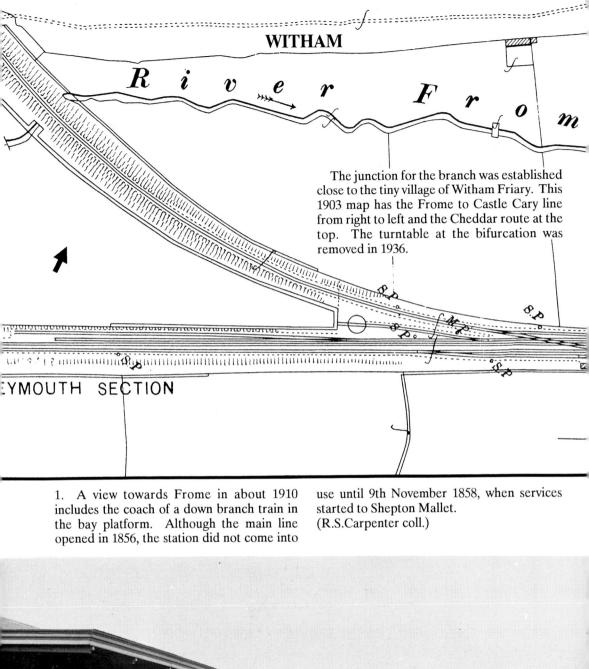

WITHAM

River From

The junction for the branch was established close to the tiny village of Witham Friary. This 1903 map has the Frome to Castle Cary line from right to left and the Cheddar route at the top. The turntable at the bifurcation was removed in 1936.

YMOUTH SECTION

1. A view towards Frome in about 1910 includes the coach of a down branch train in the bay platform. Although the main line opened in 1856, the station did not come into use until 9th November 1858, when services started to Shepton Mallet.
(R.S.Carpenter coll.)

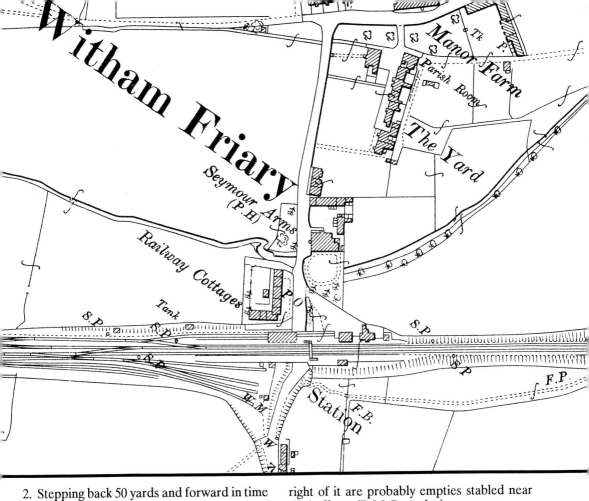

2. Stepping back 50 yards and forward in time to 24th August 1956, we witness the arrival of ex-GWR 0-6-0PT no. 3731. The coaches to the right of it are probably empties stabled near the buffers. (R.M.Casserley)

3. A westward view includes the original down platform waiting room, a sheeted luggage trolley, the goods shed and the junction signals. To end confusion with Witham in Essex, the station was belatedly renamed Witham (Somerset) in timetables from 9th June 1958. (Lens of Sutton)

Witham	1903	1913	1923	1933
Passenger tickets issued	13015	8797	7388	5703
Season tickets issued	-	-	48	54
Parcels forwarded	22913	26142	14136	1257
General goods forwarded (tons)	125	158	68	274
Coal and coke received (tons)	410	323	401	111
Other minerals received (tons)	636	328	91	33
General goods received (tons)	1115	849	898	83
Trucks of livestock handled	37	60	60	33

4. The water supply for branch engines is evident but the water column is hidden by no. 7921 *Edstone Hall*, as it speeds towards London with a parcels train on 27th October 1962. (C.L.Caddy)

5. The roof over the bay did not last until the end of branch passenger services but one of its supports was retained and fitted with a lamp bracket. The shed on the right was for parcels by passenger train. (Lens of Sutton)

6. Class 2 2-6-2T no. 41208 arrives with a train from Yatton in the last summer of branch operation. The station just outlived the branch, not closing to passengers until 30th December 1963.
(J.W.T.House/C.L.Caddy coll)

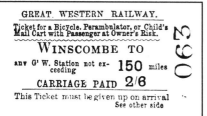

GREAT WESTERN RAILWAY.

Ticket for a Bicycle, Perambulator, or Child's Mail Cart with Passenger at Owner's Risk.

WINSCOMBE TO

any G' W. Station not ex-ceeding **150** miles

CARRIAGE PAID **2/6**

This Ticket must be given up on arrival See other side

➤

7. Seen from the inside of Witham Signal Box on 15th May 1971, class 52 no. D1053 *Western Patriarch* approaches with the 06.35 Penzance to Paddington. The box had a 67-lever frame dating from November 1942, but in later years many of these were spare. The goods yard was open for traffic until 3rd October 1966.
(G.Gillham)

8. A modified track layout was introduced on 25th June 1972. The former Cheddar Valley Bay line was extended eastwards over the site of the former up main platform to form a new connection with the main line. No. 31165 brings the Westbury to Cranmore bitumen tanks along the new line on 8th April 1976. (G.Gillham)

9. Class 35 no. D7093 runs onto the new line with a stone train on 14th January 1973. Other stone trains are berthed on the left and in the distance. (A.G.Thorpe)

10. Class 52 no. D1001 *Western Pathfinder* heads for Paddington on 20th April 1975. Earlier in the day, the railtour had been hauled from Eastleigh to Cranmore by class 9F 2-10-0 no. 92203 *Black Prince*. It was waiting to return to the ESR. (A.G.Thorpe)

11. Witham Signal Box was photographed on 6th September 1984, ten weeks before closure. The box dated from before 1880, but was extended and rebuilt in 1896. (G.Gillham)

12. No. 56045 carefully brakes its 1500 tonne train of roadstone as it slows for the junction with the West of England main line at Witham on 12th October 1984. The train is on the former Cheddar Valley branch from Merehead Quarry and is bound for Westbury sorting sidings. The colour-light signal on the right was brought into use six weeks later when the area was taken over by Westbury power box. (G.Gillham)

13. No. 50015 *Valiant* and Inspection saloon DB 999509 are pictured on 27th June 1990 at East Somerset Junction Up sidings forming the 08.33 Bristol Temple Meads to Bristol Temple Meads Inspection Special, via Westbury, East Somerset Junction, Westbury Melksham and Swindon. Personnel from the Bristol Area Civil Engineers Department are carrying out an inspection on the Merehead Branch. (S.McMullin)

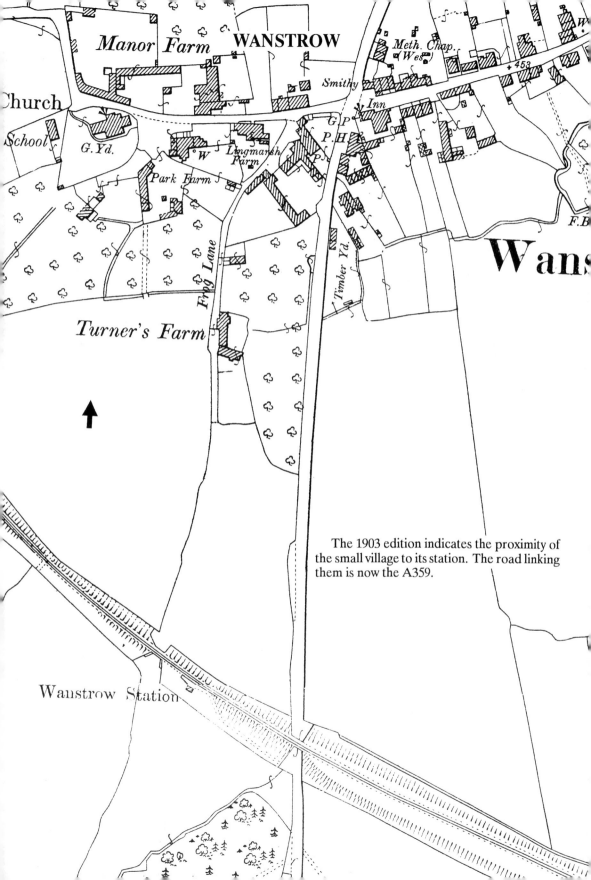

The 1903 edition indicates the proximity of the small village to its station. The road linking them is now the A359.

14. The station was opened in 1860 and seems to have had the platform ramp added later. The building bears a solitary lamp bracket. Broad gauge track materials are evident in this and the next picture; bridge rail is secured to longitudinal timbers which are tied at intervals. (Lens of Sutton)

15. A later photograph reveals reduction in the ramp inclination, enlargement of the building with incompatible materials, new lighting and speedy staff transport. The station was not staffed until 1st April 1909. (Lens of Sutton)

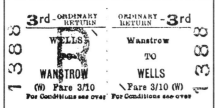

16. Owing to the scarcity of passengers in the 1930s, the GWR used diesel railcars on some journeys. This example is bound for Witham in the rain in about 1952. (M.E.J.Deane)

17. The 10.10am (Saturdays only) from Witham passes over the A359 as it arrives to collect a solitary passenger on 2nd July 1955. The sign on the two-wire pole announces *YOU MAY TELEPHONE FROM HERE* - modernisation indeed. (R.C.Riley)

18. A short goods loop and a cattle dock were opened west of the platform in January 1927. An agricultural accommodation crossing passes over the siding and main line. (Lens of Sutton)

19. A 1960 photograph features the passenger's approach, shown on the map. On the left is the later roadway to the siding which closed on 10th June 1963. (H.C.Casserley)

MEREHEAD QUARRY

20. This 1965 view towards Witham shows the siding and ground frame which were in use from 14th March 1948 until 30th April 1970. A loop, with a siding from it, was laid ¾ mile to the west and was brought into use on 31st May 1970. (C.L.Caddy)

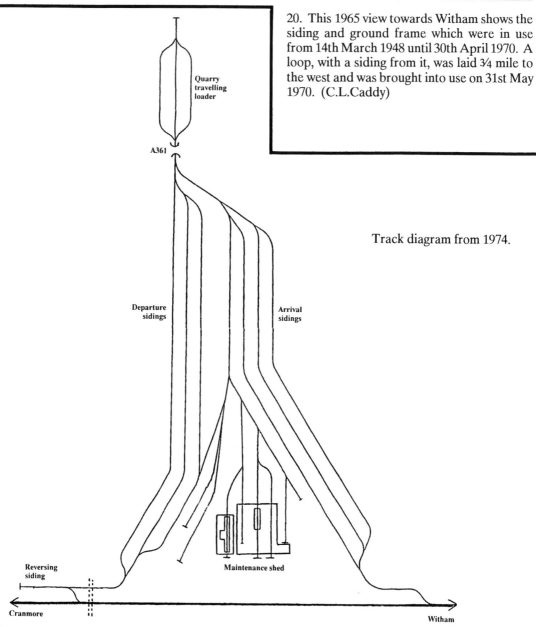

Quarry travelling loader

A361

Departure sidings

Arrival sidings

Track diagram from 1974.

Reversing siding

Maintenance shed

Cranmore

Witham

21. No. D1023 *Western Fusilier* approaches the new loop with empties in 1971. More sidings and a diesel depot were constructed behind the locomotive in subsequent years. An additional line to the quarry was laid beyond the group of trees in 1974, thus forming a triangular junction. (G.Gillham)

22. The triangular arrangement was formed by the sinuous line on the right of this picture of no. 47056 departing on 8th May 1979. The 1974 line was used for empty trains arriving. (T.Heavyside)

23. Class 9F no. 92203 *Black Prince* visited the quarry from the nearby East Somerset Railway in April 1974 and in September 1982 to undertake trials of strength. It is seen on the latter occasion with a load of 2100 tons, claimed to be a record for steam in Britain. This view of the travelling stone loader and the sidings was later restricted by screening panels. (D.Shepherd)

24. The junction of the 1974 line (behind the camera in picture 22) was recorded on 28th August 1984 as no. 50647 takes empties to the quarry. The locomotive had suffered loss of power on the 1 in 66 up from Wanstrow. No. 56045 was summoned from Westbury to assist at the rear. No. 33034 is waiting with bitumen tanks from Cranmore and two empty Seacow hoppers from the ESR. The ground frame closed on 24th November 1984, when Westbury took control of the area. (S.McMullin)

25. Propelling loaded wagons into one of the three departure roads on 9th September 1987 is General Motors *Western Yeoman II*. Note the choice of couplings. The class 59 in the background will propel its train upon departure and then reverse beyond the trees. (T.Heavyside)

26. Foster Yeoman Ltd held an open day on 26th May 1989 and displayed their fleet of General Motors class 59s. In the centre is no. 59005 which was named *Kenneth J. Painter* that day. (G.Gillham)

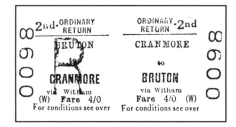

27. A platform was constructed for the open day and a shuttle service was provided to and from Westbury. This special was formed of class 108 DMUs nos B961 and B970. The platform was still in place in 1996. (G.Gillham)

28. A southward view from the road bridge in October 1995 has the three arrival roads on the left and the three departure lines on the right. The centre track leads to the maintenance shed seen in picture 26. (P.G.Barnes)

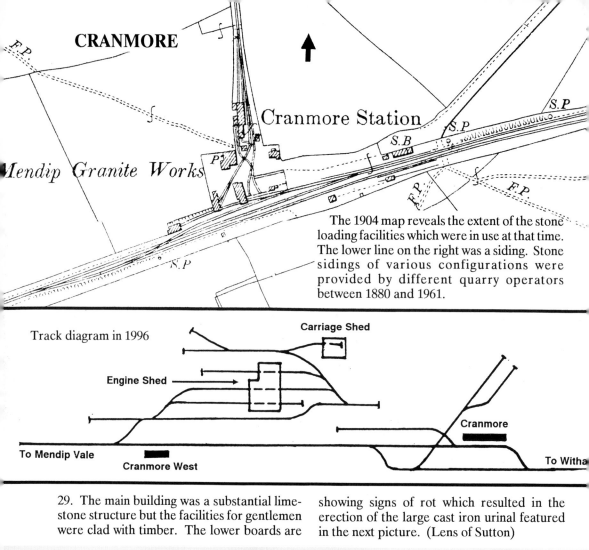

CRANMORE

Cranmore Station

Mendip Granite Works

S.B

S.P

The 1904 map reveals the extent of the stone loading facilities which were in use at that time. The lower line on the right was a siding. Stone sidings of various configurations were provided by different quarry operators between 1880 and 1961.

Track diagram in 1996

Carriage Shed

Engine Shed

Cranmore

To Mendip Vale

Cranmore West

To Witha

29. The main building was a substantial limestone structure but the facilities for gentlemen were clad with timber. The lower boards are showing signs of rot which resulted in the erection of the large cast iron urinal featured in the next picture. (Lens of Sutton)

30. Only the platform on the left existed in the broad gauge era but there were sidings on both sides of the single line. The loop and down platform came into use on 1st June 1880. (Lens of Sutton)

31. The driver of an up train walks back to the signal box with the single line tablet pouch, not long before line closure. Tarpaulins inexplicably litter the down platform. (J.W.T.House/C.L.Caddy coll)

32.
The addition of two sidings north of the station necessitated the provision of a diamond crossing in the original one. Bitumen tankers are seen in the 1904 sidings in 1965. General goods traffic ceased on 17th January 1966 but the signal box closed on 19th May 1963. (C.L.Caddy)

East Somerset Railway Reincarnation

Wildlife and railway artist David Shepherd bought class 9F no. 92203 and class 4 no. 75029 from BR at the end of steam and helped to establish a steam centre in Hampshire - see *Branch Lines to Longmoor* pictures 90-92. Following its demise in 1971, much of the stock was stored at Eastleigh until moved to Cranmore on 18th November 1973, by which time a new locomotive shed was ready. The locomotives ran under their own power at night, hauling assorted rolling stock.

33. The bitumen sidings can be seen on the right as class 33 no. D6501 leaves with empty tankers on 24th April 1972. The train usually ran thrice weekly but ceased in 1985. (G.Gillham)

34. No. 92203 *Black Prince* was recorded on 26th August 1974 while giving footplate rides near the fine new GWR-style shed. Posed in the doorway is ex-SR "Schools" class no. 928 *Stowe*, devoid of some vital linkages. It had been on display at Beaulieu Motor Museum and had been towed from Eastleigh by no. 92203 but later moved to the Bluebell Railway for restoration. (G.Gillham)

35. Brake van rides were being provided by Hunslet 0-6-0ST no. 68005 on 7th May 1979, while an ex-LBSCR class E1 0-6-0T stood on one of the new shed roads. Built at Brighton as no. 110 in 1877, the SR renumbered it B110 and sold it to a colliery in 1927. The BR number shown is thus fictional. (T.Heavyside)

36. On 9th September 1987, no. 68005 was raising revenue with a much longer train, which is obscuring the Cranmore West platform. Access to this was via the path between the wire fences and the crossing by the hut. (T.Heavyside)

37. The original buildings were artistically enhanced and subsequently photographed in 1995. The house beyond them was built in 1974 and beyond it is the 1991 building. The platform was extended at that time to accommodate five coaches. The ESR trains could not use the station until 23rd June 1985, following the cessation of bitumen traffic. (P.G.Barnes)

38. Completed in 1991, the building includes a spacious buffet, shop, art gallery and offices. A wide stairway leads from the entrance (right) up to the platform, where shelter is provided by a canopy. The materials came mainly from Lodge Hill station and Wells Priory Road goods shed. (M.Turvey)

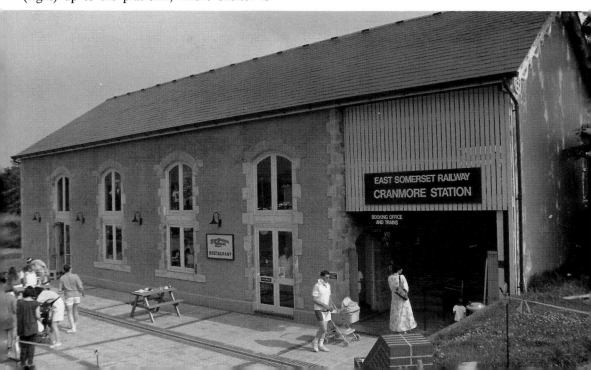

39. The signal box serves as an art gallery, with a museum on the ground floor. It was photographed on 20th November 1993, as class E1 no. B110 waits to leave with passengers that had alighted from a railtour. (V.Mitchell)

40. On the same day, the west end of the new shed was recorded from the platform of Cranmore West. This could be used when the original platform was occupied by a visiting train from BR. On the left is a 1937 Barclay 0-4-0ST carrying the fictitious GWR no. 705. The colour light signals are interlocked with the foot crossing gates. (V.Mitchell)

41. The east end of the shed and workshops was pictured in the company of no. B110 on 1st October 1994. The workshop had come from Devonport Dockyard and the smoke vents from Westbury shed. The boiler of ex-GWR 0-6-2T no. 6634 is on the ground. (M.Turvey)

Stop

Await instructions

42. Well equipped workshops allow most repairs to be undertaken. In October 1995, smokebox replacement was in progress on *Lord Fisher*, a Barclay 0-4-0ST built in 1915. (P.G.Barnes)

43. Class 4 no. 75029 passes a green flag as it backs towards its train on 1st October 1995. Standing between the former goods yard sidings is an ex-Zambesi Sawmills Railway 4-8-0 and an ex-Rhodesian Railway sleeping car, both having a gauge of 3ft 6ins. They were moved to the car park in 1996. (P.G.Barnes)

44. Amongst the interesting collection of rolling stock to be found at Cranmore in 1995 was this 0-4-0ST, built by Barclay in 1920. Hidden out of traffic was BR's only all-plastic coach, very durable but ironically suffering from a rusting underframe. (P.G.Barnes)

45. Operation was extended to a point near the former Doulting stone siding on 4th April 1980 but the platform was not completed until the following year. The site was close to the summit of the route. Doulting siding was in use from prior to 1877 to 1938. No. 92203 *Black Prince* stands at the short platform in May 1982. The eastern point was removed after the station ceased to be used in 1985. (ESR coll.)

46. Further extension took place on 23rd June 1985 when a loop two miles from Cranmore came into use. As at Merryfield Lane, there was no public access. A maximum length train waits to return to Cranmore on 20th November 1993. (V.Mitchell)

47. No. 75029 runs round its train on 1st October 1995 after having climbed to the summit at 1 in 70 and then descended at 1 in 56. Further tree clearance was in progress. (P.G.Barnes)

EAST OF SHEPTON MALLET

48. No. 5553 is hauling the 12.8pm Wells to Frome on 5th October 1951; the last coach is passing over the Somerset & Dorset line, south of Shepton Mallet Charlton Road station. The two sidings visible pass under steel spans and can be seen more clearly in picture no. 105 in our *Bath to Evercreech Junction* album. (S.C.Nash)

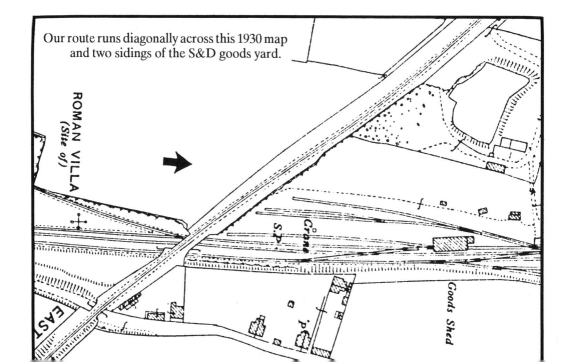

Our route runs diagonally across this 1930 map and two sidings of the S&D goods yard.

ROMAN VILLA
(Site of)

S.P.

Crane

Goods Shed

EAST

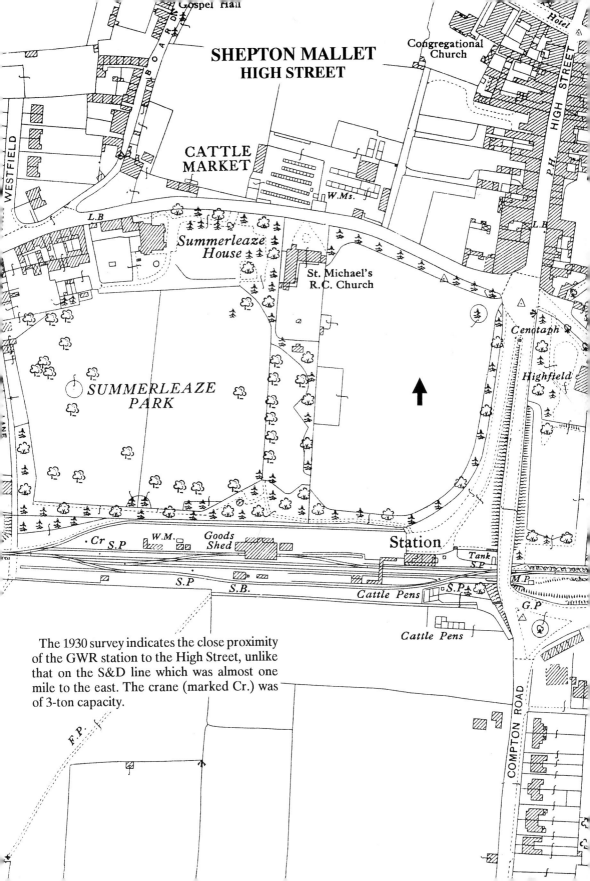

SHEPTON MALLET
HIGH STREET

Gospel Hall

Congregational Church

Hotel

HIGH STREET

P.H.

CATTLE MARKET

W.Ms.

WESTFIELD

L.B

L.B

Summerleaze House

St. Michael's R.C. Church

Cenotaph

Highfield

LANE

SUMMERLEAZE PARK

Cr S.P

W.M.

Goods Shed

Station

Tank
S.P

M.P.

S.P

S.B.

Cattle Pens

S.P

G.P

Cattle Pens

The 1930 survey indicates the close proximity of the GWR station to the High Street, unlike that on the S&D line which was almost one mile to the east. The crane (marked Cr.) was of 3-ton capacity.

F.P.

COMPTON ROAD

49. Less common architectural features are a pitched roof on the footbridge and an integral rainwater gutter. The stock present includes a horse box and four-wheeled coaches. The main building was still standing in 1996 but the yard was occupied by industrial premises. (Lens of Sutton)

50. Ex-GWR 0-6-0PT no. 4647 waits at the down platform in about 1957, while a representative of British Road Services stands on the dock once used for the transfer of the horse-drawn carriages of the gentry. (J.W.T.House/C.L.Caddy)

Shepton Mallet	1903	1913	1923	1933
Passenger tickets issued	29631	25010	18584	6308
Season tickets issued	-	-	35	88
Parcels forwarded	24139	23144	16935	15924
General goods forwarded (tons)	16580	15121	835	462
Coal and coke received (tons)	9378	9273	2778	1536
Other minerals received (tons)	545	697	384	173
General goods received (tons)	12634	11777	6682	2897
Trucks of livestock handled	265	625	440	271

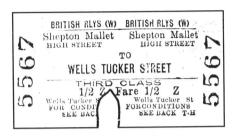

51. No. 9968 waits to depart for Witham at 7.19pm on 16th July 1960. The paved area of track on the left facilitated the cleaning of cattle wagons after unloading. The population was 5620 in 1961. (T.Wright)

52. This picture was taken a few minutes after the previous view and features the 7.20pm departure for Yatton. The grimy locomotive is class 3 2-6-2T no. 82033, a type introduced by BR in 1952. (T.Wright)

53. We can see through the goods shed in this westward view; goods traffic ceased on 13th July 1964 but stone trains from Dulcote Quarry (three miles distant) continued to pass through until October 1969. The signal box closed on 3rd May 1965. (Lens of Sutton)

54. The cattle pens are visible beyond the gas lamp in this 1963 panorama. The suffix "High Street" had been added on 26th September 1949. Note that signalling allowed up trains to start from either platform. (C.L.Caddy)

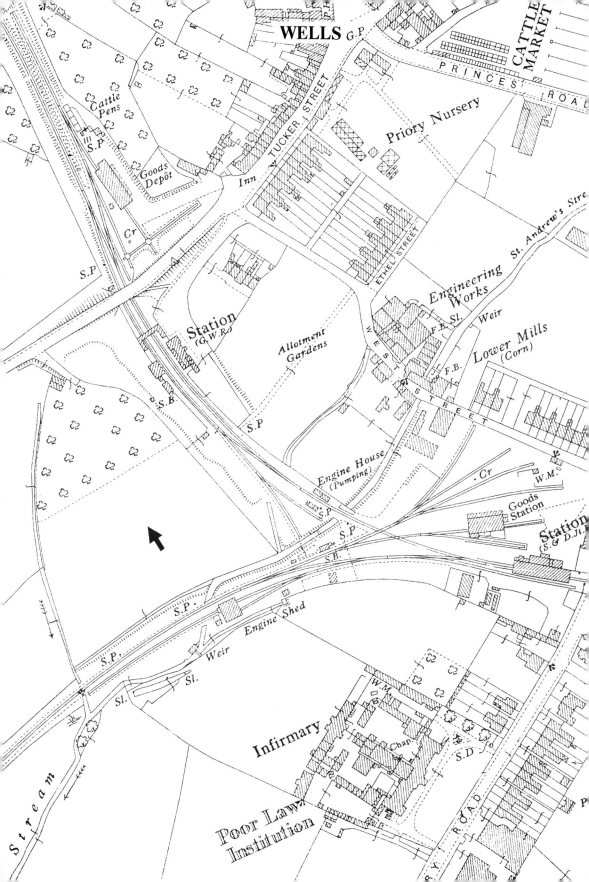

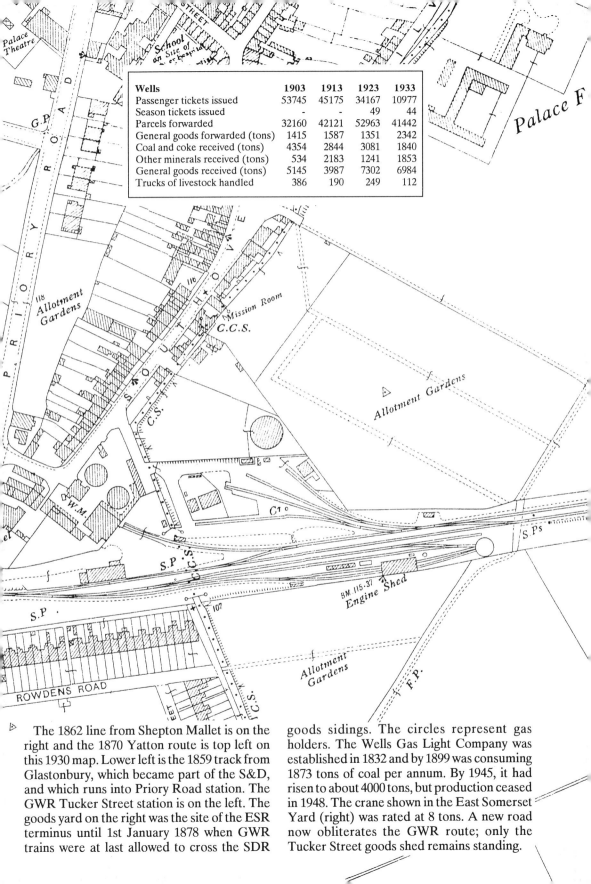

Wells	1903	1913	1923	1933
Passenger tickets issued	53745	45175	34167	10977
Season tickets issued	-	-	49	44
Parcels forwarded	32160	42121	52963	41442
General goods forwarded (tons)	1415	1587	1351	2342
Coal and coke received (tons)	4354	2844	3081	1840
Other minerals received (tons)	534	2183	1241	1853
General goods received (tons)	5145	3987	7302	6984
Trucks of livestock handled	386	190	249	112

The 1862 line from Shepton Mallet is on the right and the 1870 Yatton route is top left on this 1930 map. Lower left is the 1859 track from Glastonbury, which became part of the S&D, and which runs into Priory Road station. The GWR Tucker Street station is on the left. The goods yard on the right was the site of the ESR terminus until 1st January 1878 when GWR trains were at last allowed to cross the SDR goods sidings. The circles represent gas holders. The Wells Gas Light Company was established in 1832 and by 1899 was consuming 1873 tons of coal per annum. By 1945, it had risen to about 4000 tons, but production ceased in 1948. The crane shown in the East Somerset Yard (right) was rated at 8 tons. A new road now obliterates the GWR route; only the Tucker Street goods shed remains standing.

WELLS
EAST SOMERSET YARD

55. This westward view from 1st September 1961 has the sidings to the goods yard on the right and the 1879 engine shed on the left. Priory Road signal box is in the distance. (R.S.Carpenter)

57. Class 2 2-6-0 no. 46517 has just run over Priory Road level crossing on 13th June 1959 and is passing the remains of the platform of the ESR terminus. There had been a roof over the track and the building was used for goods traffic in its later years; see the earlier map in *Burnham to Evercreech Junction*. Sidings for a Ministry of Food depot were laid, east of the yard and south of the running line, in 1942. They were in place until 1966. (R.E.Toop)

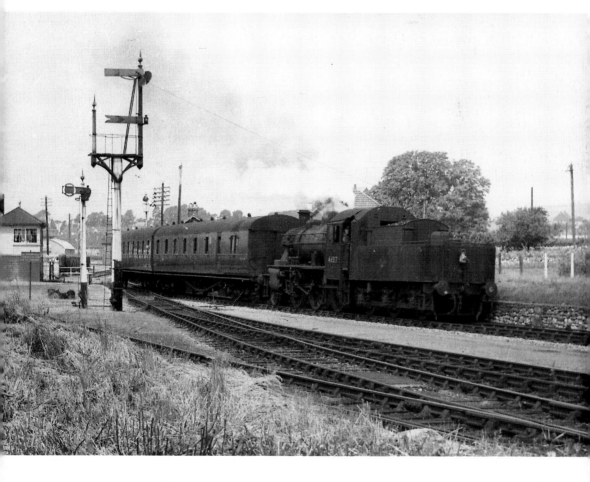

56. Looking in the opposite direction on the same day, it is evident that one section of roof remained in place. In 1961 there were three drivers, four firemen, one passenger engine and another for goods. (R.S.Carpenter)

WELLS
PRIORY ROAD

58. LMS 0-4-4T no. 1303 is approaching the S&D goods shed. On the left are the crossings so deplored by the Railway Inspectorate. A GWR coach is in one of the Tucker Street sidings. The term "Priory Road" was employed from 1883. (Lens of Sutton)

Other photographs of this station can be found in *Burnham to Evercreech Junction,* **nos 87 to 98.**

59. The station is seen from the level crossing on 2nd October 1951 after ex-LMS 0-4-4T no. 58046 had arrived from Glastonbury. Such terminating trains had to retire to the goods yard (as in the previous picture) to avoid obstructing trains on the ex-GWR route. GWR trains did not stop at this station until 1st October 1934. (S.C.Nash)

60. The Glastonbury branch closed completely on 29th October 1951 and the roof was soon removed. After that date all Western Region trains passed through without stopping, as witnessed on 27th July 1963. The ex-S&D goods yard was in use until 13th July 1964, access being via the curve on the left of this picture. Reversal was then necessary. (E.Wilmshurst)

WELLS
TUCKER STREET

61. Opening on 5th April 1870, the station was completed in a period of flamboyant Victorian architectural detailing, when artistic trimmings were given to ridge tiles, barge boards and even chimney pots.
(Lens of Sutton)

From an SR excursion handbill.

WELLS.

The old-world City of Wells is situated in the heart of the Mendip Country and has preserved its medieval buildings practically unspoiled, of which the lovely Cathedral is an outstanding example.

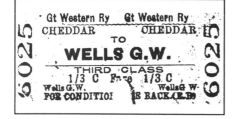

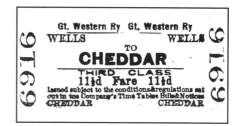

62. Our journey to Yatton continues on trains designated "up". It appears that both platforms date from the broad gauge era in view of the wide space between the tracks. The up platform waiting room seems to be of a later date. (Lens of Sutton)

63. The guard tosses a parcel into the luggage compartment of *BRISTOL DIVISION TRAIN 10* on 21st April 1934 as no. 5514 waits to depart for Witham at 12.34 pm. The 4500 class was well suited for the stiff gradients of the route. (H.C.Casserley)

64. Only one of the fine chimney pots could be seen on 2nd October 1951 as class 2251 no. 2258 waits while the signalman gives his instructions. The first signal box had been badly sited; it was between the bridges on the down platform. (S.C.Nash)

65. Water columns were provided between the tracks at both ends of the platforms, water being pumped from a stream into a tank to supply them. On the right are the two carriage sidings; the one on the left served an engine shed until 1876 and the other included a turntable until 1927. The points at the end of the down platform were for a private siding for A. Sheldon & Sons; it was in use from 1936 to 1966. (Lens of Sutton)

66. The exterior was recorded in 1958, by which time the suffix "Tucker Street" had been dropped. It was in use from 12th July 1920 until 29th October 1951. The city had only 7150 residents in 1961. (R.M.Casserley)

67. The RCTS ran the "Cheddar Valley Scenic" from Paddington on 31st May 1969. It ran to Cheddar, via Witham, reversed and then returned to London via Taunton and various lines in Bristol. The line between Cheddar and Dulcote Quarry closed officially on 26th April 1969. All three goods yards at Wells closed on 13th July 1964. (R.E.Toop)

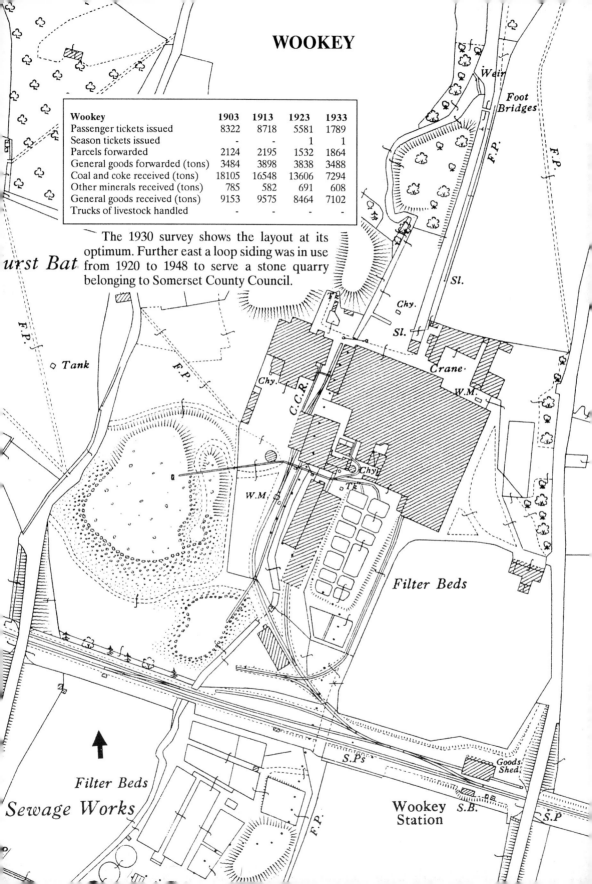

WOOKEY

Wookey	1903	1913	1923	1933
Passenger tickets issued	8322	8718	5581	1789
Season tickets issued	-	-	1	1
Parcels forwarded	2124	2195	1532	1864
General goods forwarded (tons)	3484	3898	3838	3488
Coal and coke received (tons)	18105	16548	13606	7294
Other minerals received (tons)	785	582	691	608
General goods received (tons)	9153	9575	8464	7102
Trucks of livestock handled	-	-	-	-

The 1930 survey shows the layout at its optimum. Further east a loop siding was in use from 1920 to 1948 to serve a stone quarry belonging to Somerset County Council.

urst Bat

Weir

Foot Bridges

F.P.

F.P.

F.P.

Sl.

Chy.

Sl.

Crane

Tank

F.P.

Chy.

C.C.R.

W.M.

Chy.

Tk

W.M.

Filter Beds

Filter Beds

Sewage Works

S.Ps

Goods Shed

Wookey Station

Wookey S.B.

S.P

F.P.

68. The goods shed stood devoid of track in August 1964, as a monument to past expectations of substantial traffic. The connection to the paper mill was usable from 1879 to 1965. (C.L.Caddy)

From an SR excursion handbill.

69. The signal box was set forward to give good visibility under the bridge. There was a ground frame at the west crossover. Only the goods shed and road bridge were still standing in 1996. (Lens of Sutton)

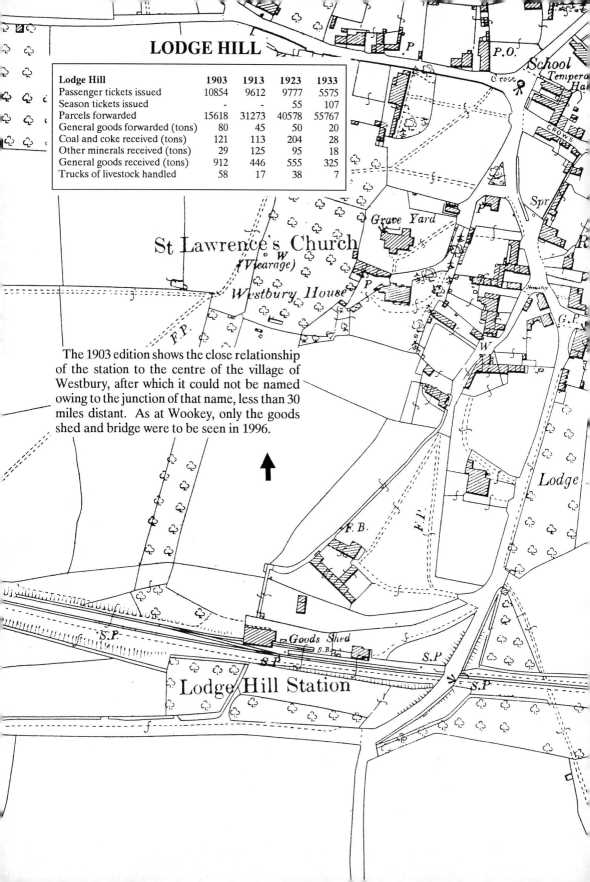

LODGE HILL

Lodge Hill	1903	1913	1923	1933
Passenger tickets issued	10854	9612	9777	5575
Season tickets issued	-	-	55	107
Parcels forwarded	15618	31273	40578	55767
General goods forwarded (tons)	80	45	50	20
Coal and coke received (tons)	121	113	204	28
Other minerals received (tons)	29	125	95	18
General goods received (tons)	912	446	555	325
Trucks of livestock handled	58	17	38	7

St Lawrence's Church
(Vicarage)

Grave Yard

Westbury House

The 1903 edition shows the close relationship of the station to the centre of the village of Westbury, after which it could not be named owing to the junction of that name, less than 30 miles distant. As at Wookey, only the goods shed and bridge were to be seen in 1996.

Goods Shed

Lodge Hill Station

70. The station approach road and some fine architectural details are included in this eastward view. Note, in particular, the variety of tiles employed and that the bridge was for double track. Westbury housed only 544 souls in 1961. (Lens of Sutton)

71. Class 2 2-6-0 no. 46517 passes through on 2nd July 1960 with a westbound freight. One wagon stands in the goods yard which closed on 10th June 1963. The station was named after a 200ft mound on the edge of Westbury Moor. (R.E.Toop)

DRAYCOTT

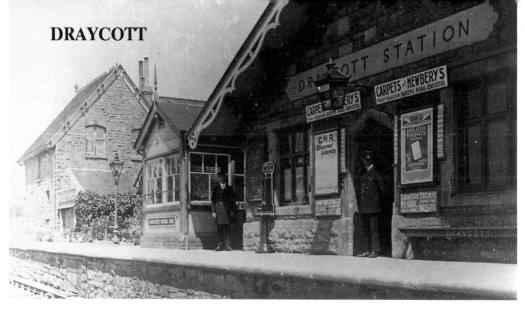

72. The signal box finial complemented the proportions of the chimney pots on the station house, while the rodding tunnel to the box was fitted with a door, an uncommon feature. Both the house and the station were in residential use in 1996. (Lens of Sutton)

Draycott	1903	1913	1923	1933
Passenger tickets issued	9720	8532	7717	3340
Season tickets issued	-	-	57	41
Parcels forwarded	12345	21140	25480	4576
General goods forwarded (tons)	406	408	255	161
Coal and coke received (tons)	343	687	724	199
Other minerals received (tons)	132	55	7	22
General goods received (tons)	637	509	336	184
Trucks of livestock handled	2	-	-	19

73. The small goods yard and the signal box were both taken out of use on 9th March 1963. The white structure once carried a loading gauge. Electric lights had replaced the oil ones seen in the previous picture. (Lens of Sutton)

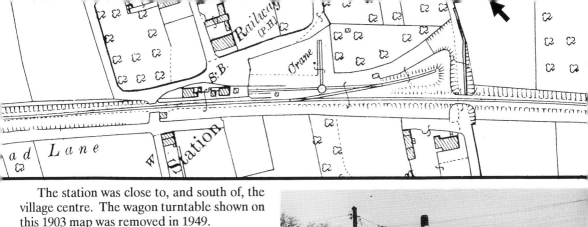

The station was close to, and south of, the village centre. The wagon turntable shown on this 1903 map was removed in 1949.

74. Low sun on 21st March 1960 enables us to see that the signal box contained a wheel for working the level crossing gates. The signs clearly state the functions of each building. (R.M.Casserley coll.)

75. Five rods were required in connection with the gates and their locks but the lane served only a few cottages. Fruit boxes are stacked high in another 1960 view. The train crew had to open the gates by hand between 1963 and 1969. (R.E.Toop)

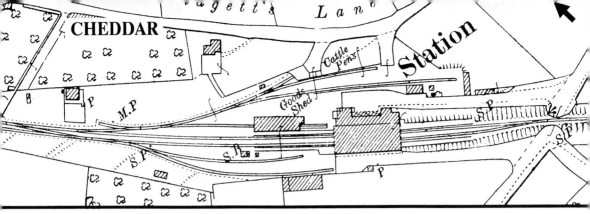

Cheddar	1903	1913	1923	1933
Passenger tickets issued	30750	25294	23001	8139
Season tickets issued	-	-	160	150
Parcels forwarded	44424	39249	31850	16626
General goods forwarded (tons)	1814	1080	4149	8829
Coal and coke received (tons)	3158	1484	2325	1352
Other minerals received (tons)	1375	408	1962	1561
General goods received (tons)	5561	3180	3432	5414
Trucks of livestock handled	274	150	151	6

Approach roads lead up to both sides of the station from the minor road that passes under the line, lower right. Not marked on this 1903 map is the 6-ton crane which was added later. Callow Rock Lime Co. siding was in use from 1922 until 1969 and was in the position of a down yard headshunt. The up yard headshunt is to the left of the single running line. Wells Cathedral Stonemasons were occupying the station building in 1996.

76. Strawberries were loaded in large quantities and conveyed in special ventilated vans fitted with generous racking. "Bournemouth" is chalked on one of the doors but many vans were sent to the Midlands overnight. The famous cheese was also distributed widely. (Lens of Sutton)

77. The 1.30pm Witham to Yatton waits under the fine roof on 24th August 1956 behind ex-GWR 0-6-0PT no. 3731. On the right is a small awning over the up entrance. The local population was 2845 at the time of closure. (R.M.Casserley)

78. The panorama from the footbridge no longer included a hanging sign for REFRESHMENT ROOM. This had closed on 19th September 1925. The wires hanging near the lamps were attached to the gas cocks. (Lens of Sutton)

CHEDDAR.

The tremendous chasm or canyon to which nothing in England can compare is more than a mile in length, with a winding road between the vast inaccessible slopes, and over-hanging gigantic masses of rock, crowned by the "Lion Rock" 500 feet high, to the top of the Mendips' south-western ridge. The caves, discovered in 1839, vary in height and breadth, opening on either side of the entrance passage, and contain singular stalactite and stalagmite formations, the colouring of which is gorgeous, rich terra-cottas ranging up through brilliant crimsons and yellow to silvery whites.

From an SR excursion handbill.

---

79. Part of the goods shed is visible in the distance, as is the roof prop which was necessary in the final years. Neglect is evident at this end, as the Beeching axe is awaited. The roof was demolished in 1964. (Lens of Sutton)

80. The single line tablet is offered up by the signalman as class 2 2-6-2T no. 41240 leaves for Yatton on 28th May 1960. By that time the crowds visiting Cheddar Caves (one mile from the station) had shown a preference for travelling on rubber tyres. (R.E.Toop)

81. The signal box was in use until 3rd May 1965. Behind it are the up sidings of the goods yard which ceased to handle traffic on 29th November 1965. The line between Cheddar and Yatton was closed entirely on 1st October 1964. (C.L.Caddy)

82. The Mendip Hills are in the background in this southward view. The shunt signal (S) enabled trains terminating here to move over the points and reverse into the up platform for departure. The Clevedon motor trains did so, once each weekday for many years.
(Lens of Sutton)

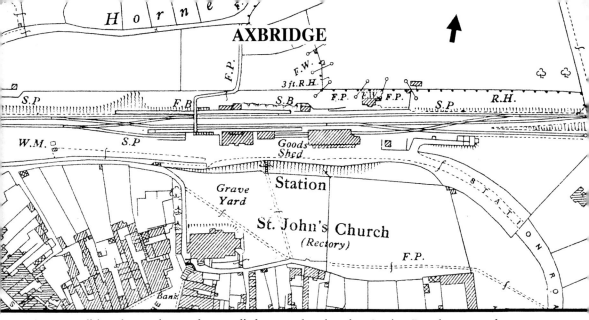

AXBRIDGE

The 1930 edition shows a layout that was little changed during the life of the line. Steps up from the churchyard gave direct access for pedestrians but Station Road was on a longer and gentler incline.

Axbridge	1903	1913	1923	1933
Passenger tickets issued	22971	15994	12606	2683
Season tickets issued	-	-	86	62
Parcels forwarded	48797	37369	32244	11434
General goods forwarded (tons)	573	514	316	147
Coal and coke received (tons)	1788	1652	1507	539
Other minerals received (tons)	3155	90	156	100
General goods received (tons)	951	3354	2424	2059
Trucks of livestock handled	259	188	74	137

83. Two postcard views illustrate that the station was built on a ledge cut into the side of the Mendips. The line drops towards Cheddar at 1 in 100 in the distance; the station masters house is in the centre. (Lens of Sutton)

84. The footbridge was extended to carry a public footpath to Fry's Hill. The signal box (right) was in use until 14th July 1907. There were 1087 inhabitants in 1961. (Lens of Sutton)

85. The loading of strawberries was labour intensive and this scene was repeated at all stations from Lodge Hill to here in season. One van is marked "Sheffield". (Lens of Sutton)

86. The 3.28pm from Witham passes between the original goods shed and the 1907 signal box hauled by 0-6-0PT no. 4647 on 8th July 1959. A pressurised oil lamp would be hoisted up the concrete post at night. (H.C.Casserley)

87. Material excavated from platform areas had been used to make up the land on the right. The goods traffic ceased on 10th June 1963, as did use of the signal box. This is a 1959 view. The Axbridge bypass now occupies the trackbed, the main building and the goods shed being at the kerbside. (H.C.Casserley)

88. The guard gives the right-away as the signalman gossips with the fireman on 27th July 1963. No. 3643 is working the 1.10pm Witham to Yatton service and has plenty of steam for the ensuing climb. (E.Wilmshurst)

89. The shelter on the left was added specially for the strawberry traffic. Beyond the outer home in the distance, the route turned north in a deep rock cutting on a 34-chain radius and an up gradient of 1 in 75. It passed through the 180yd long Shuteshelve Tunnel. (Lens of Sutton)

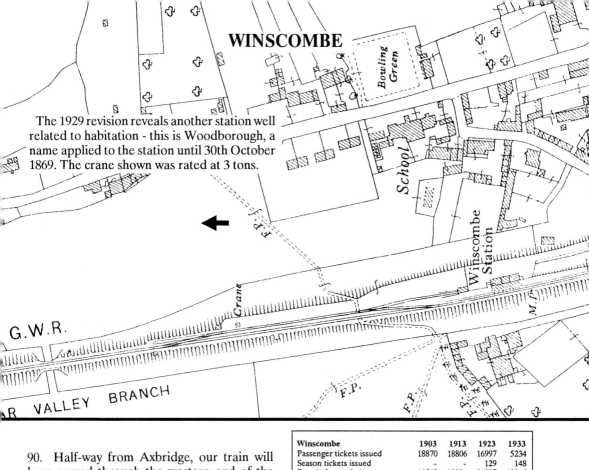

WINSCOMBE

Bowling Green

School

Winscombe Station

The 1929 revision reveals another station well related to habitation - this is Woodborough, a name applied to the station until 30th October 1869. The crane shown was rated at 3 tons.

Crane

G.W.R.

R VALLEY BRANCH

F.P.

90. Half-way from Axbridge, our train will have passed through the western end of the Mendips in Shuteshelve Tunnel. The GWR was noted for its clarity of signing. Only the platform edge was to be seen in 1996.
(Lens of Sutton)

Winscombe	1903	1913	1923	1933
Passenger tickets issued	18870	18806	16997	5234
Season tickets issued	-	-	129	148
Parcels forwarded	11569	18384	21287	12316
General goods forwarded (tons)	377	639	471	213
Coal and coke received (tons)	1055	1340	1338	980
Other minerals received (tons)	821	606	545	410
General goods received (tons)	723	2023	1628	819
Trucks of livestock handled	-	-	-	-

PARCELS OFFICE AND CLOAK ROOM

WAY OUT

BOOKING OFFICE AND WAITING ROOM

WAITING ROOM

91. This building was opened on 9th January 1905 and replaced a wooden chalet construction provided by the BER. Like many other stations on the route, a camping coach was to be found in the goods yard in many summers. The siding is in the distance. (Lens of Sutton)

92. The ground frame in the foreground ceased to be used on 10th June 1963, when freight traffic ended. This photograph was taken in August 1964, not long before the track was lifted. There were about 2500 residents at that time. (C.L.Caddy)

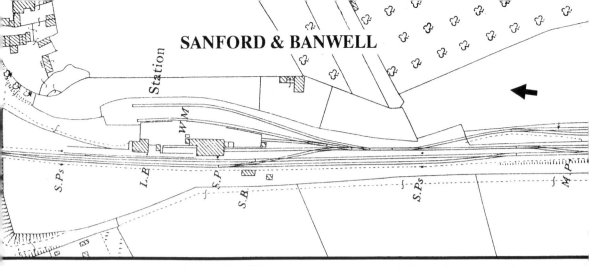

SANFORD & BANWELL

Orchards are close to the station on this 1930 map. The line passing through a gate south of the station ran for nearly a half-mile to the quarry of Roads Reconstruction Ltd. The company operated an 0-4-0 vertical-boilered Sentinel shunting engine and provided limestone for railway ballast. The firm had rail connection from 1935 to 1964; various other companies had used the sidings since they came into use in 1903. The line crossed the Sandford-Woodborough road on the level. The station building and cottage were restored in 1978 by Sandford Stone, manufacturers of ornamental garden stoneware, and can be seen by visitors to their showground.

Sandford and Banwell	1903	1913	1923	1933
Passenger tickets issued	14514	12154	10679	3941
Season tickets issued	-	-	109	111
Parcels forwarded	9116	14413	16726	4138
General goods forwarded (tons)	973	822	730	145
Coal and coke received (tons)	1384	1665	1347	66
Other minerals received (tons)	2761	82	1588	6
General goods received (tons)	1303	3471	2101	2583
Trucks of livestock handled	141	68	19	9

93. The flamboyant styling is now familiar but here there was a passing loop but only one platform. The goods loop was completed on 12th December 1905 and was in use until 1st July 1964. (Lens of Sutton)

94. Visible from a departing train on 24th August 1956 is the goods yard, which closed on 10th June 1963. The neat rockeries would soon be abandoned. The train will descend at 1 in 100 for about one mile to the almost level final section of the route. (R.M.Casserley)

95. The points opposite the 1905 signal box gave access to the goods yard, which ceased to handle traffic on 10th June 1963. The box became a ground frame on 28th October 1963. The 0-6-0PT is class 5700 no. 9615. (Lens of Sutton)

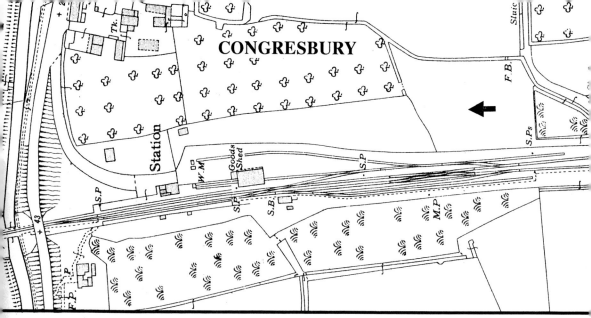

CONGRESBURY

Our route from Sandford is lower right and the line from Blagdon is above it on this 1936 map. The village was east of the station, north of which the line passed under the A370 and then over the River Yeo. Some pronounce it Coomsbury, others say Consbury and locals sometimes use four syllables. The population was 1637 in 1961.

Congresbury	1903	1913	1923	1933
Passenger tickets issued	11479	11655	8968	3477
Season tickets issued	-	-	86	38
Parcels forwarded	8625	13382	17150	1870
General goods forwarded (tons)	500	560	758	526
Coal and coke received (tons)	679	789	647	221
Other minerals received (tons)	3961	2109	201	26
General goods received (tons)	485	4879	6228	2671
Trucks of livestock handled	19	47	39	2

96. A view from the road bridge reveals that no footbridge was provided, despite the station's junction status. The road bridge has been eliminated and no evidence of the railway remains. (Lens of Sutton)

97. August 1960 and a camping coach graces the scene. Elderly coaches were adapted as holiday homes and shunted into the little used goods yards on the route from the 1930s to the early 1960s, except in the war years. (R.E.Toop)

98. No. 8746, a 5700 class 0-6-0PT, shunts an up freight on 11th March 1961. The splitting signals for the junction are in the background. The goods yard closed on 1st July 1964 but the line to Cheddar remained open for freight until 1st October of that year. (R.E.Toop)

99. The signal box and loops came into use on 14th April 1901, eight months before the branch opened. The line to Wrington curves to the left in the distance. The goods shed housed a crane of 2-ton capacity. (Lens of Sutton)

100. The 1.45pm from Yatton arrives on 27th July 1963 as the signalman approaches with the tablet; an air of neglect prevails. A house was provided for the station master; its chimneys are visible on the left. (E.Wilmshurst)

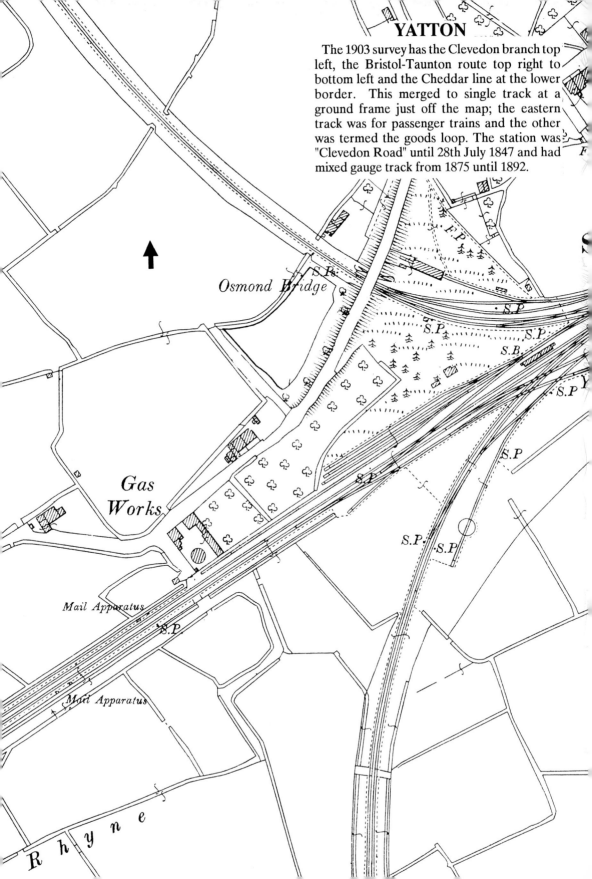

YATTON

The 1903 survey has the Clevedon branch top left, the Bristol-Taunton route top right to bottom left and the Cheddar line at the lower border. This merged to single track at a ground frame just off the map; the eastern track was for passenger trains and the other was termed the goods loop. The station was "Clevedon Road" until 28th July 1847 and had mixed gauge track from 1875 until 1892.

Osmond Bridge

S.P.

F.P.

S.P.

S.P.

S.P.

S.B.

S.P. Y

S.P.

S.P.

S.P.

S.P.

Gas Works

Mail Apparatus

S.P.

Mail Apparatus

R h y n e

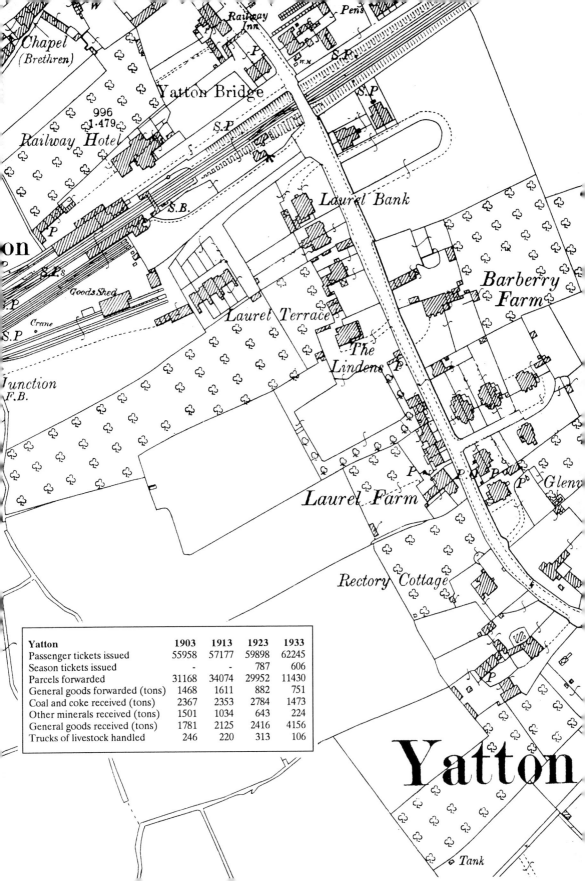

Chapel
(Brethren)

Yatton Bridge

Railway Inn

Pens

S.P.

996
1·479

Railway Hotel

S.P.

Laurel Bank

S.P.

Barberry Farm

S.B.

on

S.P.

Goods Shed

Crane

Laurel Terrace

The Lindens

Junction
F.B.

Laurel Farm

Glen

Rectory Cottage

Yatton	1903	1913	1923	1933
Passenger tickets issued	55958	57177	59898	62245
Season tickets issued	-	-	787	606
Parcels forwarded	31168	34074	29952	11430
General goods forwarded (tons)	1468	1611	882	751
Coal and coke received (tons)	2367	2353	2784	1473
Other minerals received (tons)	1501	1034	643	224
General goods received (tons)	1781	2125	2416	4156
Trucks of livestock handled	246	220	313	106

Yatton

Tank

101. A photograph from the 1930s includes a train for Wells and the Clevedon bay overall roof, which was demolished in 1956. (Mowat coll.)

102. The station gardens had a special display in 1953 for the coronation of Queen Elizabeth II. There was then a staff of over 40, which included four locomotive crews and two shedmen. (R.C.Riley)

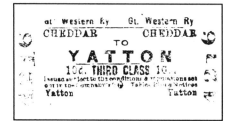

103. Class 4500 no. 5527 was recorded on 25th May 1953. The shed was west of the station and was closed on 7th August 1960. It usually housed the motive power for the Clevedon branch. (R.C.Riley)

104. While 0-6-0PT no. 7727 of 7400 class waits to leave with the 6.10pm for Witham, we can examine some of the details of the signalling and water supply. (R.M.Casserley)

105. A pannier tank takes water in August 1962 as class 2 2-6-2T no. 41245 waits on the centre siding. The main water tank is in the left background. (A.J.Pike/F.Hornby)

106. DMUs started working the Clevedon branch on 8th August 1960. One is standing in the bay on 27th July 1963 as no. D7010 speeds through, bound for Weston-super-Mare. The Clevedon branch closed on 3rd October 1966. (E.Wilmshurst)

107. A 1965 panorama has the Cheddar line on the left and the 1925 relief lines each side of the main line. The 129-lever signal box was in use from 14th April 1901 until 31st January 1972 and was designated "West" from 1925 to 1964. (C.L.Caddy)

108. The down side roadway also gave access to the goods yard. The main buildings and offices are on the up side where a ticket office was still in use in 1996. (Lens of Sutton)

109. A 1965 view shows that the middle siding and the engine release crossover (seen in picture no. 106) had been removed. Part of the goods shed is seen here and in pictures 104 and 105. The goods yard had a 6-ton crane and closed on 29th November 1965, but handled only coal in its final six months. (C.L.Caddy)

110. A stopping train from Bristol to Weston-super-Mare is pictured on 30th April 1982. By that time both bay platforms had been infilled and the footbridge had lost its roof. (T.Heavyside)

The 1 inch to 1 mile survey of 1946 includes the entire length of the branch to Blagdon.

WRINGTON VALE LIGHT RAILWAY

111. It seems that cattle grids were a novelty in 1901, as a contemporary report stated: *On each side of the crossing a shallow pit has been dug underneath and at right angles with the line of rails. Over the top of this opening iron bars are placed in the form of a grating. It is found from experience that animals do not venture across an arrangement of this kind, which is therefore, known as a cattle "fence".* A bored Peter Davey is waiting to photograph the once-a-weekday goods train at Brinsea Crossing in 1945. The result was a failure but more recently he has had success as author of *Bristol's Tramways*. (S.Miles Davey)

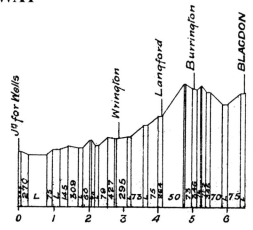

YATTON, WRINGTON, and BLAGDON.—Great Western.

Mls	Down.		mrn	mrn	mrn	aft	aft			Mls	Up.		mrn	mrn	mrn	aft	aft		
—	Yatton ....dep.	8 10	....	1150	4 10	6 50	....	....		—	Blagdon ....dep.	7 35	....	9 35	2 35	5 20	....	....
1¼	Congresbury	8 15	8 19	12 0	4 14	6 54	....	....		1¼	Burrington	7 39	....	9 39	2 39	5 24	....	....
4¼	Wrington..............	....	8 2	1211	4 22	7 2	....	....		2¼	Langford	7 43	....	9 43	2 43	5 30	....	....
5¼	Langford..............	....	8 34	1223	4 29	7 9	....	....		3¾	Wrington..............	7 49	....	9 49	2 49	5 40	....	....
6¼	Burrington............	....	3 40	1234	4 35	7 15	....	....		6¼	Congresbury 28..........	7 58	8 4	9 59	2 59	6 0	....	....
8	Blagdon ....arr.	....	8 45	12.40	4 40	7 20	....	....		8	Yatton 30, 28 ...... arr.	....	8 10	10 5	3 5	6 7	....	....

1902

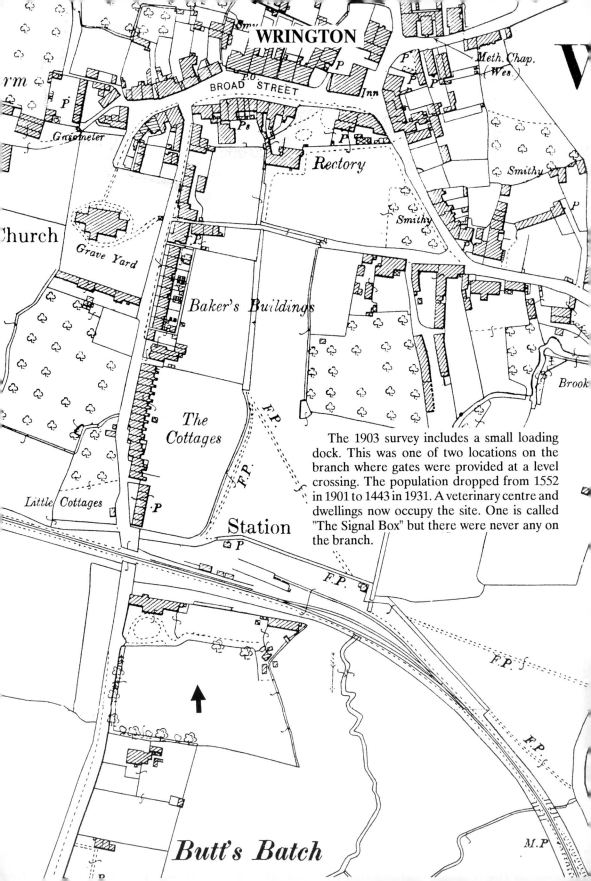

WRINGTON

Meth. Chap. (Wes.)

BROAD STREET

Inn

Rectory

Smithy

Gasometer

Church

Grave Yard

Smithy

Baker's Buildings

Brook

The Cottages

F.P.

The 1903 survey includes a small loading dock. This was one of two locations on the branch where gates were provided at a level crossing. The population dropped from 1552 in 1901 to 1443 in 1931. A veterinary centre and dwellings now occupy the site. One is called "The Signal Box" but there were never any on the branch.

Little Cottages

Station

P

F.P.

F.P.

F.P.

M.P.

Butt's Batch

112. A standard building design was employed on the branch but the materials varied; here red bricks were used. The platforms were only 2ft 6ins high. In 1926, a Mondays-only train started here at 7.38am for the benefit of weekenders needing to return to Bristol before business hours. (Lens of Sutton)

Wrington	1903	1913	1923	1933
Passenger tickets issued	11020	9462	6061	-
Season tickets issued			4	-
Parcels forwarded	3606	10128	9270	3433
General goods forwarded (tons)	309	294	265	234
Coal and coke received (tons)	1562	1487	1045	577
Other minerals received (tons)	957	118	250	7
General goods received (tons)	638	1753	1493	747
Trucks of livestock handled	13	16	56	10

113. This was the only station on the branch to have a crane. It was rated at only 30cwt (1.5 tons) and is visible near the van, which is standing on the loop. The goods yard remained open until 10th June 1963, receiving only full loads of coal in its final years. (R.M.Casserley coll.)

LANGFORD

Langford	1903	1913	1923	1933
Passenger tickets issued	7085	4534	1846	-
Season tickets issued			-	
Parcels forwarded	4989	3592	6649	579
General goods forwarded (tons)	104	204	63	18
Coal and coke received (tons)	612	23	246	41
Other minerals received (tons)	812	673	171	-
General goods received (tons)	375	374	544	101
Trucks of livestock handled	1	11	2	-

1924

The 1903 edition does not reveal that the level crossing had gates. The road later became the A38 and the occasional closure of the gates caused considerable build up of road traffic.

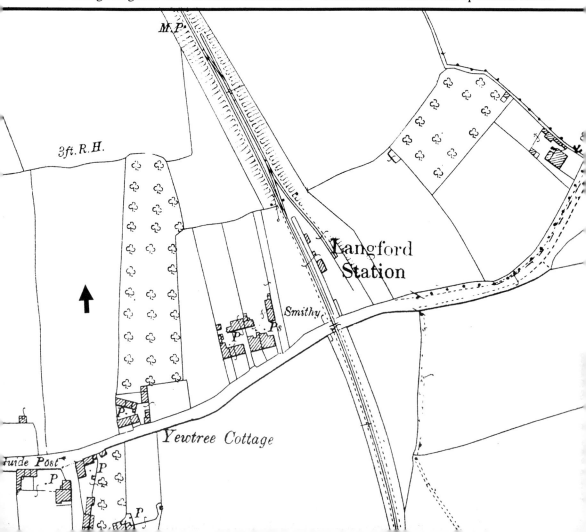

114. Only one other branch station had toilet facilities and, as at Cranmore, cast iron was the material chosen. The line southward climbed at 1 in 50. The building was demolished in 1958 but the platform and one level crossing gate post could still be seen in 1996. The gates are on the right of this original postcard view. (D.Counsell coll.)

115. Lightweight flat bottom rail spiked to the sleepers was used on most of the branch but chaired bullhead material was employed on the steep gradients, where rail creep could be a problem. The goods yard was the loading point for salvaged metal during World War II. (Lens of Sutton)

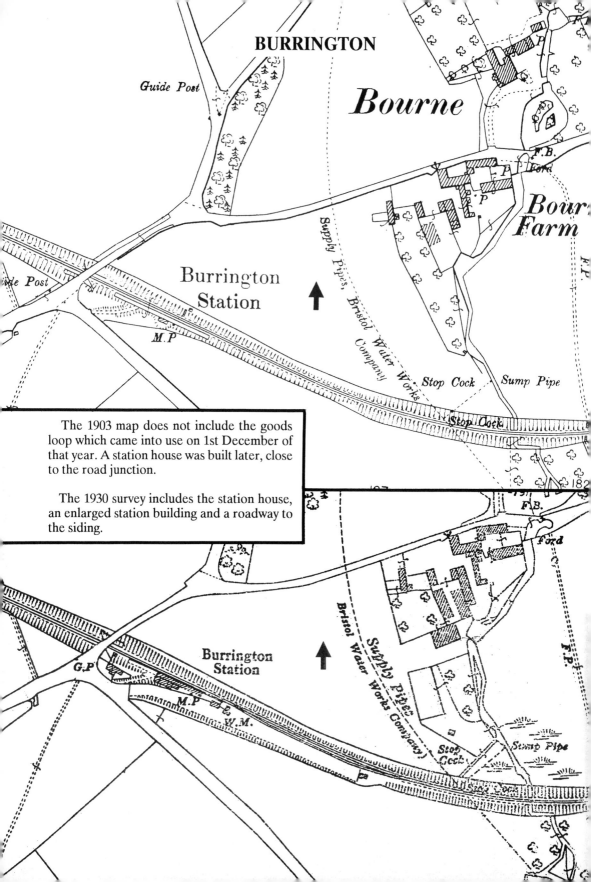

BURRINGTON

Bourne

Guide Post

*Bour
Farm*

Burrington
Station

ide Post

M.P

The 1903 map does not include the goods loop which came into use on 1st December of that year. A station house was built later, close to the road junction.

The 1930 survey includes the station house, an enlarged station building and a roadway to the siding.

Burrington
Station

G.P

M.P

W.M.

Supply Pipes, Bristol Water Company Works

Stop Cock   *Sump Pipe*

Stop Cock

F.B.
Ford

Bristol Water Works Company (Supply Pipes)

*Stop
Cock*   *Sump Pipe*

Burrington	1913	1923	1933
Passenger tickets issued	4850	2106	-
Season tickets issued		5	-
Parcels forwarded	12093	8661	615
General goods forwarded (tons)	103	200	45
Coal and coke received (tons)	386	-	94
Other minerals received (tons)	185	703	44
General goods received (tons)	838	466	141
Trucks of livestock handled	-	1	1

YATTON, WRINGTON, and BLAGDON.

Miles	Up.	Week Days.		Suns.		Miles	Down.	Week Days.		Suns.	
		mrn	aft					mrn	aft		
	Yatton ....dep.	8 15	6 40	..	..		Blagdon...........dep.	8 55	7 20	..	..
1¼	Congresbury............	8 19	6 44	....	....	1¼	Burrington...............	9 2	7 25	....	....
4¼	Wrington	8 28	6 53	..	..	3¼	Langford.................	9 6	7 29	..	..
5	Langford	8 35	7 0	....	....	3¾	Wrington.................	9 12	7 36	....	....
6¾	Burrington	8 41	7 6	..	..	6¾	Congresbury 49..........	9 23	7 46	..	..
8¼	Blagdon ....arr.	8 45	7 10	....	....	8¼	Yatton 12, 17, 47... arr.	9 28	7 50	....	....

1931

116. The goods loop is beyond the platform and remained usable until the line west of Wrington closed completely in 1950. This building was demolished in 1958 but the house remains occupied. An annual excursion was run from Bristol for many years, even after closure to regular passenger services, for pilgrims to a site nearby where the hymn "Rock of Ages" was composed in a storm. (Mowat coll.)

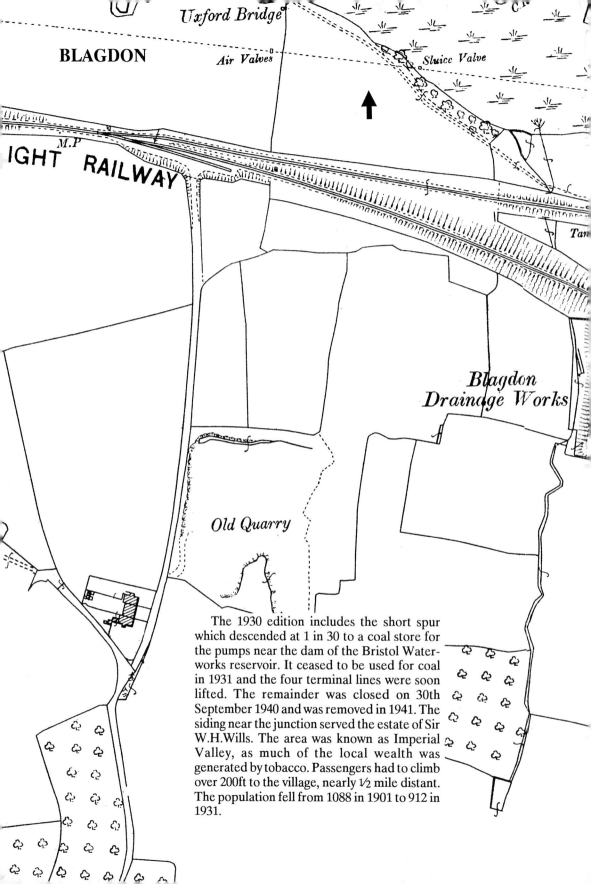

BLAGDON

Uxford Bridge

Air Valves

Sluice Valve

M.P

IGHT RAILWAY

Tan

Blagdon
Drainage Works

Old Quarry

The 1930 edition includes the short spur which descended at 1 in 30 to a coal store for the pumps near the dam of the Bristol Waterworks reservoir. It ceased to be used for coal in 1931 and the four terminal lines were soon lifted. The remainder was closed on 30th September 1940 and was removed in 1941. The siding near the junction served the estate of Sir W.H.Wills. The area was known as Imperial Valley, as much of the local wealth was generated by tobacco. Passengers had to climb over 200ft to the village, nearly ½ mile distant. The population fell from 1088 in 1901 to 912 in 1931.

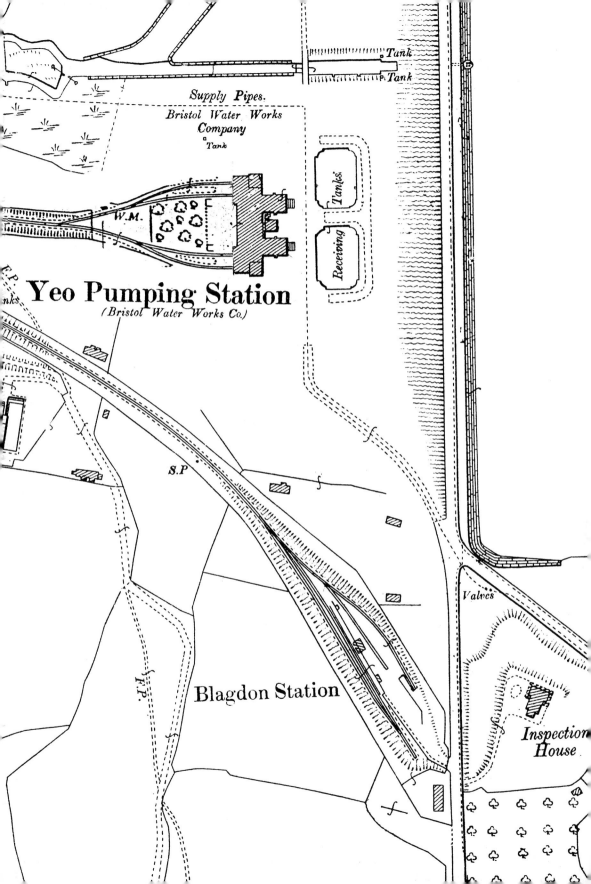

Supply Pipes.

Bristol Water Works
Company
Tank

Tank
Tank

Tanks

Receiving Tanks

W.M.

Yeo Pumping Station
(Bristol Water Works Co.)

S.P

F.P.

F.P.

Blagdon Station

Valves

Inspection
House

117. The final climb was at 1 in 75 into the station, where locomotives always ran round their trains. There were no signals, as the branch was subject to the "one engine in steam" rule. Passenger services ceased on 14th September 1931 and goods facilities lasted until 1st November 1950. The building is now a private house; a substantial two-storey extension has been tastefully executed to maintain the integrity of the original structure. (Lens of Sutton)

118. It appears that the passenger coaches have been shunted into the goods yard to enhance the composition of this posed photograph. On the right is the small goods shed. An engine was based here until 1924, but legend records that its wooden shed was destroyed by fire in 1912. There is no evidence in photographs or on maps of any such shed existing. (Lens of Sutton)

Blagdon	1903	1913	1923	1933
Passenger tickets issued	9419	6469	3407	-
Season tickets issued			4	-
Parcels forwarded	5035	17653	4035	1193
General goods forwarded (tons)	207	405	92	4
Coal and coke received (tons)	668	1942	1437	15
Other minerals received (tons)	690	53	52	-
General goods received (tons)	1032	126	172	76
Trucks of livestock handled	11	8	16	5

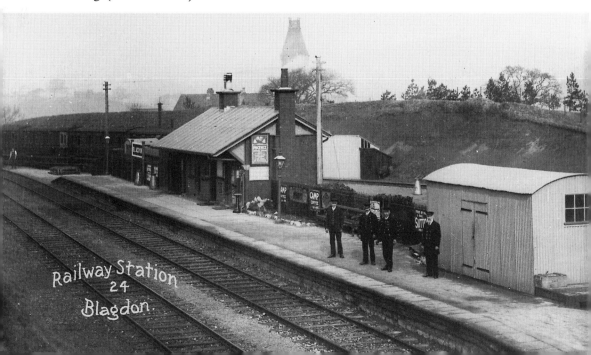

Railway Station
24
Blagdon

119. The low height of the platform is evident as we look at the rear of class 517 0-4-2T no. 540 as it waits to depart at 7.20pm on 22nd May 1929. The intricate detailing of the cast iron urinal can also be examined. The adjacent part of the building had been extended to provide facilities for ladies. Extra traffic was handled during World War II when a sack factory was set up nearby; it made sandbags until about 1948. (H.C.Casserley)

120. The white entrance gates are visible in a fine panorama of this peaceful outpost of the GWR in August 1937. The occupants of the camping coach were surrounded by trees and had the Mendip Hills in the background for the pursuit of the simple pleasures of life. (R.M.Casserley coll.)

Middleton Press

Easebourne Lane, Midhurst, W Sussex. GU29 9AZ Tel: 01730 813169 Fax: 01730 812601
If books are not available from your local transport stockist, order direct with cheque,
Visa or Mastercard, post free UK.

BRANCH LINES
Branch Line to Allhallows
Branch Line to Alton
Branch Lines around Ascot
Branch Line to Ashburton
Branch Lines around Bodmin
Branch Line to Bude
Branch Lines around Canterbury
Branch Lines around Chard & Yeovil
Branch Lines around Cromer
Branch Lines to East Grinstead
Branch Lines of East London
Branch Lines to Effingham Junction
Branch Lines around Exmouth
Branch Line to Fairford
Branch Lines around Gosport
Branch Line to Hawkhurst
Branch Lines to Horsham
Branch Lines around Huntingdon
Branch Line to Ilfracombe
Branch Line to Kingswear
Branch Lines to Launceston & Princetown
Branch Lines to Longmoor
Branch Line to Looe
Branch Line to Lyme Regis
Branch Lines around March
Branch Lines around Midhurst
Branch Line to Minehead
Branch Line to Moretonhampstead
Branch Line to Padstow
Branch Lines around Plymouth
Branch Lines to Seaton and Sidmouth
Branch Line to Selsey
Branch Lines around Sheerness
Branch Line to Shrewsbury
Branch Line to Swanage *updated*
Branch Line to Tenterden
Branch Lines around Tiverton
Branch Lines to Torrington
Branch Lines to Tunbridge Wells
Branch Line to Upwell
Branch Lines of West London
Branch Lines around Weymouth
Branch Lines around Wisbech

NARROW GAUGE
Branch Line to Lynton
Branch Lines around Portmadoc 1923-46
Branch Lines around Porthmadog 1954-94
Branch Line to Southwold
Douglas to Port Erin
Kent Narrow Gauge
Two-Foot Gauge Survivors
Romneyrail
Southern France Narrow Gauge
Vivarais Narrow Gauge

SOUTH COAST RAILWAYS
Ashford to Dover
Bournemouth to Weymouth
Brighton to Eastbourne
Brighton to Worthing
Dover to Ramsgate
Eastbourne to Hastings
Hastings to Ashford
Portsmouth to Southampton
Southampton to Bournemouth

SOUTHERN MAIN LINES
Basingstoke to Salisbury
Bromley South to Rochester
Crawley to Littlehampton
Dartford to Sittingbourne
East Croydon to Three Bridges
Epsom to Horsham
Exeter to Barnstaple
Exeter to Tavistock
Faversham to Dover

London Bridge to East Croydon
Orpington to Tonbridge
Tonbridge to Hastings
Salisbury to Yeovil
Swanley to Ashford
Tavistock to Plymouth
Victoria to East Croydon
Waterloo to Windsor
Waterloo to Woking
Woking to Portsmouth
Woking to Southampton
Yeovil to Exeter

EASTERN MAIN LINES
Fenchurch Street to Barking
Ipswich to Saxmundham
Liverpool Street to Ilford

WESTERN MAIN LINES
Ealing to Slough
Ely to Kings Lynn
Exeter to Newton Abbot
Newton Abbot to Plymouth
Paddington to Ealing
Slough to Newbury

COUNTRY RAILWAY ROUTES
Andover to Southampton
Bath Green Park to Bristol
Bath to Evercreech Junction
Bournemouth to Evercreech Jn.
Cheltenham to Andover
Croydon to East Grinstead
Didcot to Winchester
East Kent Light Railway
Fareham to Salisbury
Frome to Bristol
Guildford to Redhill
Reading to Basingstoke
Reading to Guildford
Redhill to Ashford
Salisbury to Westbury
Stratford upon Avon to Cheltenham
Strood to Paddock Wood
Taunton to Barnstaple
Wenford Bridge to Fowey
Westbury to Bath
Woking to Alton
Yeovil to Dorchester

GREAT RAILWAY ERAS
Ashford from Steam to Eurostar
Clapham Junction 50 years of change
Festiniog in the Fifties
Festiniog in the Sixties
Isle of Wight Lines 50 years of change
Railways to Victory 1944-46
SECR Centenary album
Talyllyn 50 years of change
Yeovil 50 years of change

LONDON SUBURBAN RAILWAYS
Caterham and Tattenham Corner
Charing Cross to Dartford
Clapham Jn. to Beckenham Jn.
Crystal Palace (HL) & Catford Loop
East London Line
Finsbury Park to Alexandra Palace
Kingston and Hounslow Loops
Lewisham to Dartford
Lines around Wimbledon
London Bridge to Addiscombe
Mitcham Junction Lines
North London Line
South London Line
West Croydon to Epsom
West London Line
Willesden Junction to Richmond

London Suburban Railway continued .....
Wimbledon to Beckenham
Wimbledon to Epsom

STEAMING THROUGH
Steaming through Cornwall
Steaming through the Isle of Wight
Steaming through Kent
Steaming through West Hants
Steaming through West Sussex

TRAMWAY CLASSICS
Aldgate & Stepney Tramways
Barnet & Finchley Tramways
Bath Tramways
Bournemouth & Poole Tramways
Brighton's Tramways
Burton & Ashby Tramways
Camberwell & W.Norwood Tramways
Clapham & Streatham Tramways
Croydon's Tramways
Dover's Tramways
East Ham & West Ham Tramways
Edgware and Willesden Tramways
Eltham & Woolwich Tramways
Embankment & Waterloo Tramways
Enfield & Wood Green Tramways
Exeter & Taunton Tramways
Greenwich & Dartford Tramways
Hammersmith & Hounslow Tramways
Hampstead & Highgate Tramways
Hastings Tramways
Holborn & Finsbury Tramways
Ilford & Barking Tramways
Kingston & Wimbledon Tramways
Lewisham & Catford Tramways
Liverpool Tramways 1. Eastern Routes
Liverpool Tramways 2. Southern Routes
Liverpool Tramways 3. Northern Routes
Maidstone & Chatham Tramways
Margate to Ramsgate
North Kent Tramways
Norwich Tramways
Portsmouth's Tramways
Reading Tramways
Seaton & Eastbourne Tramways
Shepherds Bush & Uxbridge Tramways
Southampton Tramways
Southend-on-sea Tramways
Southwark & Deptford Tramways
Stamford Hill Tramways
Twickenham & Kingston Tramways
Victoria & Lambeth Tramways
Waltham Cross & Edmonton Tramways
Walthamstow & Leyton Tramways
Wandsworth & Battersea Tramways

TROLLEYBUS CLASSICS
Croydon Trolleybuses
Bournemouth Trolleybuses
Hastings Trolleybuses
Maidstone Trolleybuses
Reading Trolleybuses
Woolwich & Dartford Trolleybuses

WATERWAY ALBUMS
Kent and East Sussex Waterways
London to Portsmouth Waterway
West Sussex Waterways

MILITARY BOOKS
Battle over Portsmouth
Battle over Sussex 1940
Bombers over Sussex 1943-45
Bognor at War
Military Defence of West Sussex
Military Signals from the South Coast
Secret Sussex Resistance
Surrey Home Guard
Sussex Home Guard

OTHER RAILWAY BOOKS
Garraway Father & Son
Index to all Middleton Press stations
Industrial Railways of the South-East
South Eastern & Chatham Railways
London Chatham & Dover Railway
War on the Line (SR 1939-45)